CESC
FÁBREGAS

World Cup Heroes

CESC FÁBREGAS

Tom Oldfield

JOHN BLAKE

Published by John Blake Publishing Ltd,
3 Bramber Court, 2 Bramber Road,
London W14 9PB, England

www.johnblakepublishing.co.uk

This edition published in paperback in 2010

ISBN: 978 1 84358 176 5

British Library Cataloguing-in-Publication Data:

A catalogue record for this book is available from the British Library.

Design by www.envydesign.co.uk

Printed in Great Britain by CPI Bookmarque, Croydon, CR0 4TD

1 3 5 7 9 10 8 6 4 2

Papers used by John Blake Publishing are natural, recyclable products made
from wood grown in sustainable forests. The manufacturing processes
conform to the environmental regulations of the country of origin.

Pictures reproduced by kind permission of Getty Images.

INTRODUCTION

Ask fans of Arsenal and Spain and they will tell you that Cesc Fábregas is one of the greatest players in world football today. The Gunners' midfielder, they say, is definitely one of a handful of players who will light up the World Cup in South Africa, a football genius who might well be the catalyst that sparks Spain to lift the Jules Rimet trophy.

Sir Alex Ferguson disagrees. He said that Fábregas can only be called a 'great' player when he has some silverware to prove it. And while Arsenal fans may have thought that was sour grapes, Cesc backed the Manchester United boss. He told the *Sunday Times*: 'I 100 percent agree with him. I can't say I'm a great player. And I always say at Arsenal we're a very, very good side, but not a great side. When we win something together as a group we can say we're great. You've been successful when you've won trophies. When you've won European Championships, World Cups, Premier Leagues, Champions Leagues: then you can say you're a success.'

Fábregas has certainly enjoyed some triumphant moments, not least being a key part of Spain's Euro 2008 winning side, but someone of his ability should have the trophy cabinet groaning under the weight of silverware. And that is a concern to Arsenal fans. He obviously enjoys playing under his mentor Arsène Wenger, the man who gave a rookie teenager his big break, but the team's habit of falling just short, season after season, continues to fuel speculation that the midfielder will eventually return to his home-town club Barcelona in search of those elusive medals.

On the other hand, if Fábregas and his Spanish team-mates can reproduce their qualifying form in South Africa, then he might well be able to show Sir Alex the most coveted medal of all next time they meet.

1

Francesc Fábregas Soler was born on 4 May 1987 to Francesc senior and Nuria. With his sister Carlota, the family lived in Arenys de Mar in the Maresme region of Barcelona. The small town, with a population of around 14,000, is a major fishing port with a relaxed environment. The close-knit family has always played an important part in his life and he recalls his childhood fondly.

Fábregas' father ran the family construction business that has been passed down through the generations, his mother went on to become a director of a sales company, and both have taken great pride in the way their son has blossomed into a fine professional footballer. In fact a passion for the game was in the genes. Francesc senior once had a trial with Barcelona but he was turned down and played for the Third Division side Calella.

The whole family were Barça fans. Being season-ticket holders, Fábregas was fortunate to sample the atmosphere inside the Nou Camp from a young age. Rumour has it that he was just nine months old when his grandfather Alex took him to the famous stadium for the first time. Naturally his first football kit was the Barcelona strip, one that he wore with great pride.

Fábregas saw Barça win the European Cup against Sampdoria in 1992 and two years later, when he was still only seven, he watched the club reach the 1994 Champions League final, only to see them lose 4–0 to AC

Milan. It taught him the highs and lows of football at a young age.

He still has a season ticket for the Nou Camp, which he uses when he has time off at Arsenal. He has never thought of relinquishing it, preferring to loan it out to friends than give it up. On the few occasions that Wenger grants him time off, he likes nothing better than to go home and watch Barcelona play. Barça will be his club for life.

He was probably around nine years old when he first heard of Arsenal Football Club and his main memories of that team were Tony Adams and David Seaman. His favourite player though was the Spanish midfielder Josep Guardiola, a classy passer of the ball. The fact that Fábregas now wears the number four shirt for Arsenal is a tribute to Guardiola, who wore the same number in his days at Barça.

As a schoolboy, Fábregas played against boys several years older than him. This toughened him up. The pitches were rarely of good quality and he always ended up with nasty cuts and bruise when he fell. But he relished the challenge of outwitting stronger opponents, and it taught him the value of being an intelligent as well as a skilful player. He learnt to make a pass quickly to avoid rough tackles, although he was not afraid to put his boot in. Even today, despite his relatively slight frame, it is noticeable that the Spaniard shows no fear in the tackle and he does his fair share of grafting in midfield.

People soon started to take notice as he starred for his local side Mataro. But even when he was attracting the attention of professional clubs, he still thought his future lay in the family construction firm. But when Barcelona revealed their interest in signing Fábregas for their youth system, he knew it was the chance of a lifetime. He was still only 10 years old and he had the world at his feet.

Combining his studies with the training schedule at Barcelona proved tricky and gave Fábregas little time to himself. As he recalled in an interview with the *Daily Mail*: 'I had to wake up early in the morning, go to school, come back, have lunch, rest a little bit, go running, then a taxi was coming to pick up about six of us and take us to training at Barcelona. We would train at 7.30pm, finish at 9.30pm and take a taxi home again. Then I would have to do my homework, sometimes to 2am or 3am and wake up early again to go to school. It was like that for five years, really hard.'

Many young hopefuls see the standard of their school work decline as they pursue a career in football, but Fábregas showed equal commitment to his studies. Speaking to the *Daily Mail* in 2007, he said, 'I never did something like... how do you say? Truant. Maybe sometimes I was thinking about it, but I knew I would feel bad afterwards, so I never did it. In the end I got all my exams and good grades. Now I can speak Spanish, Catalan, English and a little bit of French.'

Lionel Messi was one of the youngsters training at the same time as Fábregas and the little Argentine holds the Barcelona youth system, called the cantera, in the highest esteem. As he told John Carlin in the *Observer Sport Monthly*: 'The Barcelona youth programme is one of the best in the world. As a kid they teach you not to play to win, so much as to grow in your ability as a player. At Barça we trained every day with the ball. I hardly ever ran without a ball at my feet.' Matches for the Barcelona youth sides were generally heavily one-sided. Fábregas recalls the team winning a string of emphatic victories with score-lines that sometimes resembled rugby results.

Fábregas made excellent progress and was soon in the Spanish squad for the FIFA Under-17 World Cup in Finland in 2003. The tournament put young players in front of a worldwide audience, showcasing them to the top clubs. There are always plenty of scouts at such events, hoping to discover the 'next big thing'. Knowledgeable Spanish supporters raved about Cesc's talent. Elsewhere, though, he was relatively unknown. The sudden media attention that followed his international call-up came as something of a surprise to him; it was a new experience, as was the fact that each of Spain's games would be televised for fans back home. The players were frequently asked for autographs and Fábregas was only too happy to oblige. He just hoped the team could live up to their expectations.

He need not have worried. Spain enjoyed a terrific tournament and he was central to their success, pulling the strings and popping up to score from midfield, winning the Golden Boot award with six goals. In the semi-final against Argentina, Fábregas went head-to-head with Messi, his Barcelona colleague, in what proved to be a thrilling contest between two excellent sides. Spain won in extra-time finale and Fábregas still recalls the match with great pride, telling *FIFA.com*: 'In that game we were 2–0 down in the first half, but we went on to win in the last minute of extra time.'

Even though Spain were beaten 2–0 in the final against Brazil, Fábregas was named the World Cup Golden Ball winner, awarded to the tournament's best player. It had been a remarkable, even life-changing, spell and he returned to his club with renewed self-belief and a bigger appetite for success.

Fábregas was enjoying his time at Barcelona and saw his game improve week by week, but he was realistic and questioned whether he would receive a first-team opportunity at the club, considering the enormous talent of the first-team squad. Frustrated and concerned that he would be frozen out at Barcelona, he was uneasy. So when the Arsenal manager Wenger revealed his interest in bringing Fábregas to London he felt he could not turn him down.

It was certainly not an easy decision. He told the media: 'At Barça we played Arsenal a few months before in a youth tournament and we beat them 5–1. I scored two goals and felt, I don't want to go because we are better. But then they made me the proposal and I saw that Arsenal was a great club. I came to see the training ground and to talk to Mr Wenger. He impressed me a lot. I had something in my mind saying, "Go on, you have to sign because everything is going to be fine."'

And so, in July 2003, Cesc Fábregas completed his move from Barcelona to Arsenal. At just 16 years of age, it was a brave decision.

2

The club arranged accommodation for Fábregas in north London. He and Philippe Senderos, the Swiss central defender, lived with an Irish landlady called Noreen. She helped the pair come to terms with the English lifestyle and gave them a safe, happy base in which to relax away from football. As he became more confident, he spent more time exploring the city.

Former Arsenal defender Martin Keown tells a funny story from Cesc's early days at the club. He told the *Sunday Mirror*, 'I remember meeting his mother and she was about the same age as me. I thought, "It's about time to get out now!" When you're older than your team-mate's mother, the writing is definitely on the wall!'

At 16 Fábregas expected to work his way up through the youth system over the next few seasons, but Wenger had other ideas and he soon realised that his journey to first-team football would be far shorter than he could ever have imagined. But in the meantime the Arsenal coaching staff told him in no uncertain terms that he needed to improve his defensive skills. 'We signed you because you are good technically, but if you don't defend you cannot play for Arsenal,' they would say. So he worked on that part of his game.

Fábregas remembers those early days well, telling the *Daily Mail*: 'My very first match for Arsenal was against Coventry, away, in the Under-17s. My family came and it was freezing cold. My dad came, my grandparents, two uncles and two aunts and they were all freezing as well.' It was hardly an auspicious start, but things soon improved, even if the weather did not. His performances for the Under-17s caught the eye of the coaching staff and he began to feature for the reserves, too. He was still very slight and needed to bulk up but his talent was unquestionable.

Fábregas watched as the Gunners marched towards an unbeaten league season in 2003-04. The likes of Thierry Henry, Robert Pires and Patrick Vieira produced incredible consistency and even the previous champions Manchester United had no reply. Although he did not feature in the Premiership, Fábregas was given opportunities to shine in the Carling Cup, a competition in which Wenger always gave his youngsters first-team experience. So Cesc made his Arsenal debut at home to Rotherham on 28 October 2003 in the third round.

He had to wait until 2 December for his next taste of first-team action. The Carling Cup fourth-round draw paired the Gunners with Wolverhampton Wanderers, again at Highbury. Wenger kept his promise to test out some of his younger players, selecting Fábregas in midfield alongside Patrick Vieira. To play alongside his club captain was a special moment for the young Spaniard and, desperately seeking to impress, he certainly made the most of it. Vieira helped Fábregas throughout the game, giving advice and encouragement, just as he did on the training ground.

Arsenal were leading 4–1 when Fábregas enjoyed one of the most memorable moments of his career. In the right place at the right time, he stabbed home a loose ball with two minutes to go. It was his first goal for the club. Wenger was delighted with his display and, back home, his family beamed with pride. It was a special night. Most people his age had only finished their GCSEs that summer but he was playing, and scoring, in front of more than 28,000 people at Highbury.

Fábregas had played well enough to feel legitimately disgruntled at the decision to drop him to the bench for the Carling Cup quarter-final, away to West Brom. It was all part of a learning process. The Gunners were already 2–0 ahead when Wenger sent him on with 15 minutes to go. Victory meant another chance to shine as Arsenal looked forward to a semi-final with Middlesbrough.

The two sides faced each other four times in less than a month in the New Year. While the Gunners dominated the Premiership and FA Cup clashes, winning both games 4–1, Boro enjoyed success in the Carling Cup matches. Sadly for Fábregas, he did not take part in either contest and the second-string line-up missed his assured passing in midfield. Trailing 1–0 after the first leg, Wenger threw a few more first-team players into the return match, but it was not to be. Middlesbrough won 3–1 on aggregate and Fábregas was denied the possibility of appearing in a showpiece final.

The Gunners soon had the Premiership title wrapped up, but their bid for an unbeaten league season persuaded Wenger not to throw his youngsters into league action. The regulars were given the chance to finish what they had started and, after a 2–1 win on the last day of the campaign against Leicester, Arsenal celebrated going through an entire Premiership season without defeat.

Fábregas spent the summer reflecting on the incredible progress he had made during the 2003-04 campaign. It had been a superb season: making his Arsenal debut, scoring his first goal for the club, playing alongside Patrick Vieira. Little did he know that Wenger would have much bigger plans for him when the new campaign kicked off.

3

There was limited transfer activity for the Gunners over the summer months, causing some concern among those who wanted big-name signings. Wenger seemed happy to put his faith in the talented youngsters coming through the youth system and, of course, there was Reyes, who had only just arrived from Sevilla in January and was still adjusting to life in the Premiership. It was a boost for Cesc Fábregas that his manager had so much confidence in his young charges, and he hoped he would have a chance to force his way into Wenger's plans.

The worry for Arsenal fans was that their rivals had invested heavily during the summer in order to stop a repeat of the last season's rout. Manchester United announced their intention to win back the title by signing teenage sensation Wayne Rooney from Everton for an initial £20 million. Chelsea's owner, Roman Abramovich, brought in Jose Mourinho who wasted little time in making his mark with a string of new arrivals, including Arjen Robben and Didier Drogba.

Nonetheless, Fábregas was confident. It remained to be seen how many appearances he would make over the course of the season, but he looked around the team and felt sure the Gunners could defend their title. The big concern was Patrick Vieira's future. The Frenchman had clearly been tempted by an offer from Real Madrid and could not make up his mind whether to stay at Highbury.

The FA Community Shield (previously called the Charity Shield) has rarely provided clues to the coming season. But the clash between champions Arsenal and rivals Manchester United was an entirely different affair. It showed just how bright the Gunners' future would be as Wenger unleashed several talented youngsters in front of a large television audience for the first time.

Fábregas was delighted to be named in the starting line-up for the match at the Millennium Stadium in Cardiff. Surrounded by fellow fledglings, it would be a big test of the club's next generation and Cesc wanted to show that he belonged out there. Wenger had no qualms about throwing his youngsters into the fray against Roy Keane and company. And they did not let him down. They turned on the style in a breathtaking display of pace and movement to leave United shell-shocked as the Gunners completed a comprehensive 3–1 victory.

While Fábregas' compatriot Jose Antonio Reyes was the star of the show, his own efforts did not escape his manager's notice. Wenger told the press: 'To play like he did against a team of United's quality at 17 is fantastic.' As Michael Hart observed in the *Evening Standard*: 'Fábregas, just 17 and given the task of deputising for Vieira, played with such composure, thought and maturity to suggest he will develop into an outstanding midfield player.' And the Arsenal fans even created a special song for Cesc: 'He's only 17, he's better than Roy Keane.'

As the league season began, it was clear that Fábregas had convinced Wenger that he was ready to step up to the first team on a regular basis. At just 17 years and 103 days he became the youngest Premiership debutant in the club's history, away to Everton at Goodison Park, where he impressed everyone as he helped his team-mates achieve a comfortable 4–1 victory. Far from being overawed by the occasion, Fábregas was prominent in midfield and the absent captain Vieira was hardly missed. Wenger was immensely proud of his fledgling midfielder and said, 'We had a 17-year-old and a 35-year-old in Dennis Bergkamp and they both showed that age does not matter. As long as you have intelligence and technique, then that is enough.'

Question marks remained over how often Wenger would use the youngster, especially considering the other stars in the Arsenal squad. But the Frenchman showed a lot of faith in him, selecting him in the starting line-up again for the home game against Middlesbrough. Fábregas helped the Gunners recover from 3–1 down to win 5–3, stretching Arsenal's unbeaten league run to 42 games and, in the process, equalled Nottingham Forest's long-standing record.

While it might have seemed natural for Wenger to rest Fábregas in the midweek game against Blackburn, the Gunners boss did no such thing. Fábregas again proved pivotal as Arsenal eventually broke down a stubborn Rovers side. The youngster missed a decent chance in the first half, but was at the heart of their best moments in the second period as Arsenal won 3–0. It had been a great start to the season: Arsenal had gone past Forest's record and sat proudly at the top of the table.

A trip to Norwich gave Fábregas his fourth consecutive league start. More glorious attacking football allowed the Gunners to cruise to a 4–1 victory as four different players scored. Such was Cesc's progress he now had international commitments to consider as he continued to shine for the Spanish Under-21 side and his displays marked him out as an exceptional young talent.

Back at Arsenal, Fábregas eventually got a rest as Vieira returned from injury against Fulham. It was another victory. The Gunners were making everything look so simple and their unbeaten league run showed no signs of being brought to an end. Would Arsenal be able to win back-to-back league crowns?

On 17 September, Fábregas was finally able to put pen to paper and signed a contract with the Gunners until 2009. English law meant he had not been able to do so before, but he was only too happy to commit to the club, telling the media: 'My first year here has been like a dream. I never thought I would have the opportunity to play in the first team so soon. I am very excited for my future.'

The next few weeks were a little subdued as Fábregas had to accept a fringe role. On 2 October, Wenger restored him to the starting line-up, giving him the chance to impress at Highbury against Charlton. While the teenager put in another promising shift, it was Henry who stole the show as he scored twice, once with an audacious back-heel into the bottom corner. Fábregas was quickly becoming a firm favourite with the Arsenal supporters and the Spaniard loved the atmosphere inside the stadium.

His solid display ensured he kept his place for the visit of Aston Villa two weeks later. Fábregas again fitted in perfectly with the pass-and-move football the Gunners loved to play and a 3–1 win did not tell the whole story of Arsenal's dominance. He never seemed to waste the ball or make the type of rash decisions one might expect from a youngster. He always knew where his team-mates were and found them with unerring accuracy.

The Spaniard was pleased to get his first Champions League outing under his belt in midweek against Panathinaikos. A 2–2 draw was a satisfactory result, but the Gunners failed to unleash their full artillery of attacking football. Fábregas was paired with Edu in midfield and the duo complemented each other well. However, some nervy defending and a lapse from Jens Lehmann cost Arsenal two points that night in Greece. It was an eye-opening experience for the youngster as he saw the differences between football in the Champions League and the Premiership. Invariably, the Gunners found it much tougher to play their flowing passing game in Europe.

Wenger then named him among the substitutes for the trip to Old Trafford for a massive clash with Manchester United. If Arsenal avoided defeat, they would reach the incredible tally of 50 games unbeaten in the league. It was amazing that the computer had served up the contest at this point on the fixture list. Naturally, United were desperate to be the team to deny the Gunners that record and the match simmered throughout. A tight, physical contest ended in misery for Arsenal as United won 2–0.

Arsenal's unbeaten streak was over and, to make matters worse, Fábregas and his team-mates appeared unable to come to terms with the defeat. The hangover from the loss sent the Gunners' season spiralling out of control. For some reason, Wenger and his players appeared to take defeat more ungraciously than other sides and Ferguson branded them 'the worst losers of all time.' From players surrounding the referee and protesting at decisions on the pitch to bitter post-match interviews, Arsenal were not winning many friends.

From leading the Premiership and looking imperious, Arsenal suffered a worrying dip. It was hard for anyone connected with the club to put their finger on what had changed or what was going wrong, but fixtures against weaker sides suddenly became trickier than usual. It was all very annoying, but Fábregas and the rest of his Arsenal colleagues were pleased to relieve some of their Old Trafford frustration with a 2–1 midweek victory over Manchester City in the Carling Cup.

Sloppiness marred the last game of October and then November began with a 1–1 draw at home to Panathinaikos. The Gunners' ruthless streak had deserted them. Usually so prolific at home, many predicted the floodgates would open once Henry handed them the lead from the penalty spot, but Arsenal failed to put the game beyond their opponents. Panathinaikos eventually drew level with 15 minutes remaining as Pascal Cygan inadvertently deflected a long-range shot past Lehmann.

Another draw, this time away to Crystal Palace, did little to lift the gloom in the Gunners camp and gave plenty of encouragement to the rest of the Premiership and Chelsea, taking advantage of the Gunners' rotten form, ended the day two points clear at the top of the table.

4

Arsenal needed to regroup and their youngsters gave them a boost when they beat Everton 3–1 in the Carling Cup, then the first-team regulars recorded an incredible 5–4 victory over Tottenham to lift the mood around the club. It was one of the most enthralling matches of Cesc's short career. After going 3–1 up, the Gunners should have sealed the match, but again defensive frailties were exposed. Cygan, Sol Campbell's replacement, was struggling to adapt to English football and opposition teams sensed that the back four were a shadow of their former selves. Panic quickly spread through the team but they just about managed to hang on for the much-needed three points.

November ended with a 2–1 defeat at Anfield against Liverpool. More points dropped against their rivals angered the Gunners and Fábregas knew that Mourinho was rubbing his hands with glee. Fortunately the new month breathed fresh life into the Gunners. Although Wenger's fledglings lost to Manchester United in the Carling Cup, the first-team regulars returned to top form as Arsenal put together a good run of results, starting with a 3–0 home win to Birmingham. They even secured a place in the second round of the Champions League after Fábregas scored against a poor Rosenborg side, putting him in the record books yet again – this time as Arsenal's youngest ever goal-scorer in Europe.

The hammering of Rosenborg was the perfect preparation for Chelsea's visit to Highbury. The challengers and the champions squared up to each other in a match that received major hype from Sky Sports. Wenger and Mourinho would stand toe-to-toe and Fábregas would get a chance to ruffle the feathers of Frank Lampard, Claude Makelele and company. Fábregas was involved early as he laid the ball forward and it eventually fell for Henry, who gave Arsenal the lead inside two minutes. The Blues had been caught cold. In the past, the Gunners would have powered on but, without Vieira and low on confidence, they allowed the Blues back into the game. Chelsea exploited the home side's newly acquired inability to deal with set pieces as John Terry headed home an equaliser.

A quickly taken free-kick from Henry restored Arsenal's advantage, but Mourinho tinkered with his formation at half-time and got instant results as Chelsea powered their way back into the game. Again it came from a set piece, Eidur Gudjohnsen looping the ball into the net. Both sides might have snatched a winner, but in the end had to settle for a 2–2 draw. Arsenal had missed their chance to gain ground on the leaders, and the Blues left Highbury with even greater confidence in their ability to last the pace at the top.

Fábregas was given a rest as Vieira returned to the midfield against Portsmouth at Fratton Park where a goal from Campbell was enough to earn a 1–0 victory. For some reason, the complacency and erratic performances then returned to blight Arsenal over the next few weeks. A 1–1 draw at home to Manchester City meant that Chelsea's lead at the top stretched to seven points. The momentum was undoubtedly with the Blues. A 2–1 win over Stoke saw Fábregas and a youthful Arsenal side begin their FA Cup campaign in positive fashion. With any dreams of the Premiership title slipping from their grasp, Arsenal were looking to other competitions for a more realistic chance of silverware.

Bolton once more proved to be the Gunners' bogey team. Sam Allardyce seemed to have discovered the right approach against Wenger's passing style. Fábregas played just over one hour of the contest before making way for Reyes but the Trotters hung on to an early lead and put another massive dent in the Gunners' title bid. Fábregas remained on the bench during a welcome 1–0 win over Newcastle but hoped to be back for the next round of the FA Cup. They were playing Wolves, a game that brought back fond memories for Cesc who had opened his goal-scoring account for Arsenal against them. The Gunners won 2–0, but he only came off the bench for the final 15 minutes.

If he had been disappointed to be left out of the line-up to face Wolves, one can only imagine his agony at being named as a substitute for the clash with Manchester United. Fábregas had been desperate to play in such a huge contest, but perhaps Wenger felt that his temperament was not ready for the type of heated clash it promised to be at Highbury. Maybe it was the correct decision. It was no secret the two sets of players disliked each other, but nobody could have predicted that the animosity would start in the tunnel, before the match even kicked off. Patrick Vieira and Roy Keane, the two captains, were involved in a simmering argument over something the Arsenal skipper had allegedly said to United defender Gary Neville as the teams headed to the changing rooms after the warm-up.

Fábregas took his place on the bench and was soon celebrating, though, as Vieira put Arsenal ahead. Ryan Giggs equalised for United 10 minutes later as the match swung from end to end and tempers came to the boil. Wayne Rooney was fortunate to stay on the pitch after several clattering challenges and a mouthful of abuse directed at the referee. To Cesc's delight, Highbury was rocking again when Dennis Bergkamp pounced to send the Gunners in at half-time with a 2–1 lead.

But, after the interval, Keane began to dominate midfield

and his team-mates responded. Cristiano Ronaldo fired home an equaliser and, with the Gunners looking shell-shocked, the Portuguese winger scored again four minutes later from Giggs' cross. Mikael Silvestre was sent off with 20 minutes remaining and Arsenal pushed forward in search of a way back into the game. Fábregas was finally brought on in the last 10 minutes but, by then, the Gunners had become desperate, resorting to a more direct style of play. In the end United found the knockout blow as John O'Shea placed an exquisite chip over Almunia to seal a 4–2 win for the visitors.

Before the match, Wenger had admitted that whoever lost this fixture would be out of the title race and, true to his word, he told the media that the Premiership trophy was now out of reach for Arsenal. Suddenly, the FA Cup and Champions League took on an even greater significance for Fábregas and his team-mates.

5

Despite the disappointment of a failing Premiership challenge, there was no point in the Arsenal players feeling sorry for themselves. They simply had to get on with the job and they did just that away to Aston Villa. Fábregas was again left on the bench until the final 10 minutes, but was relieved to see his colleagues put the game to bed with three goals in the first half hour. With Edu and Vieira performing well in the centre of midfield, Fábregas had to be patient and wait for his chance. It was a difficult spell for the Spaniard. He would have to get used to a substitute's role in the coming weeks. And things were complicated by the fact Fábregas had to deal with reports about his parents getting a divorce. It was all pretty upsetting and left him shaken.

A 5–1 victory over Crystal Palace at Highbury saw Fábregas used as a late substitute once again in an Arsenal squad of 16 that did not contain a single Englishman. But he was relieved to be back in the starting line-up for the FA Cup-tie against Sheffield United at Highbury. It was a below-par Arsenal performance and a late penalty earned the visitors a replay at Bramall Lane. For Fábregas, it had not been the return he was hoping for, although he offered occasional glimpses of his talent and forced a good save from United goalkeeper Paddy Kenny.

The teenager found himself on the bench again for the Champions League second-round, first-leg match against Bayern Munich, and could only sit and watch as Arsenal put in a shambolic display. They were fortunate to come away with only a 3–1 defeat and faced a tough task in the second leg at Highbury. It had been a cold and frustrating night for the Spaniard. Watching his team-mates crumble on a chilly night in Munich, Fábregas was left downbeat. An injury to Edu before half-time had forced a substitution, but Wenger opted to send on Flamini. Fábregas had done little wrong during the season and was disappointed to see his first-team appearances suddenly limited.

On 5 March, a morale-boosting win at home to Portsmouth gave the team some much-needed confidence ahead of the return match with Bayern. With over an hour gone, Wenger sent Fábregas into the fray and the substitution bore fruit immediately. Lifted by his creativity and that of fellow replacement Pires, Arsenal took the lead on the night through Henry. It made it 3–2 on aggregate to Bayern, but one more goal for the Gunners would put them through on away goals. Hard though they tried, Fábregas and his team-mates could not find that elusive goal. The game ended 1–0 and Arsenal were out.

They shifted their focus to the FA Cup, the only trophy left to play for. Of all the teams they could have faced they drew Bolton. On this occasion, though, Arsenal stayed strong. They were helped by an early goal and then El-Hadji Diouf's foolish red card for elbowing Lehmann. Wenger was determined not to put too much of a burden on Cesc's still developing body so he was an unused substitute, but was relieved that the dream of making it to the Millennium Stadium was becoming a real possibility.

Fábregas played the full 90 minutes at Blackburn as Arsenal kept up their pursuit of second spot in the league. Van Persie scored the winner after a delightful build-up involving Fábregas and Cole. Cesc was everywhere, tackling back one minute and shooting for goal the next. Once again he was

showing Wenger that he could handle the pressure of English football. It was a good win against a stubborn Rovers side.

Two more Premiership wins, over Norwich and Middlesbrough kept the Gunners on course for second place. The 4–1 win over Norwich at Highbury was emphatic and reminded everyone of the gulf between the teams at the top and bottom. Having played half of the Norwich game, Fábregas put in another good display away to Middlesbrough and was part of the move that led to Arsenal's winning goal.

The importance of the FA Cup semi-final against Blackburn on 16 April was not lost on Fábregas. The competition represented the Gunners' final chance to salvage something from their season. The clash with Blackburn proved a typically physical contest. As one would expect from a team containing the likes of Lucas Neill, Andy Todd and Paul Dickov, Rovers were not shy to throw themselves into challenges. Fábregas began among the substitutes, but joined the action just after half-time, replacing Ljungberg. Pires put Arsenal ahead after 42 minutes, but the match remained tight as Cesc and company failed to make the most of their chances. Fábregas was guilty of a couple of misses but, just as importantly, he kept his cool in the heated atmosphere. Van Persie secured the team's place in the final with two goals in the last four minutes as Blackburn pushed for an equaliser.

Back in the league, Chelsea were 11 points clear of Arsenal who were challenging for second place. The Gunners missed a late chance to reduce the gap on the leaders when they drew 0–0 with Mourinho's side at Stamford Bridge. Fábregas was selected in midfield and stood his ground against more experienced opponents, and it was a good sign that Arsenal were able to emerge with a point against the soon-to-be champions.

The Gunners' consistency was impressing everyone. A 1–0 victory over Tottenham gave the Arsenal fans plenty to cheer about, with Reyes grabbing the winner after receiving an inch-perfect pass from Fábregas. His vision had unlocked a stubborn Spurs defence. Then a 2–0 win at West Brom was followed by a superb 3–1 triumph over Liverpool at Highbury in a memorable match for Fábregas. The Spaniard set up the team's second goal for Reyes and then sealed the victory by scoring the third himself, finishing a typically fluent Arsenal attack after Bergkamp's assist. It was an important victory over a side that would go on to snatch the Champions League title in a penalty shoot-out later that month.

Things got even better for the Gunners in midweek as they turned on the style against Everton, winning 7–0 before losing 2–1 to Birmingham, finishing in second place. And then came the FA Cup final.

6

Cesc Fábregas could not wait to sample the atmosphere inside the Millennium Stadium on FA Cup final day. Manchester United would undoubtedly be tough opponents. Ferguson's side had won both the league matches during the season and revenge was definitely on the menu.

The bad news for Arsenal came in the form of Henry's enforced absence due to injury. It caused Wenger to rethink his tactics and decide on a more defensive 4-5-1 formation, leaving Bergkamp up front on his own. Fábregas received the verdict that he had been praying for. He was in the starting line-up, playing alongside Vieira and Gilberto in central midfield. It was a rather negative approach from the Gunners, but the Spaniard agreed with Wenger – the team would do whatever it took to lift the cup.

The walk out onto the pitch at the Millennium Stadium was something Cesc would never forget – the excitement, the nerves, the emotions. With both teams using the same formation, a predictable stalemate ensued. Rooney and Ronaldo caused major problems for the Gunners' full-backs and Fábregas found himself spending a lot of time chasing back and helping the defence. There was so little space in the central midfield areas and the Spaniard found it tough to get into his usual rhythm. Arsenal created little going forward and were grateful to Lehmann for keeping them in the contest with several good saves.

A frustrating afternoon for Fábregas ended after 86

minutes when Wenger took him off and brought on van Persie. He had worked diligently for the cause, but it was not the type of flowing match he enjoyed Arsenal seemed to decide that a penalty shoot-out was their best chance of victory and played even more negatively during extra-time. The cup would be decided by spot-kicks for the first time in its history.

Lehmann became Arsenal's hero that afternoon, making the decisive save, pushing aside Scholes' penalty. Vieira netted the winning kick and the Arsenal celebrations began. Fábregas had won his first medal at the club. It was an incredible feeling as he joined in the lap of honour and he could not wait to get his hands on the famous trophy. It was undoubtedly one of the most exciting days of his life. But his breakthrough season was not over yet though. Selected as part of the Spanish squad for the Under-20 World Cup, he headed off to Holland for the tournament.

In truth, the long, arduous campaign in England left Fábregas a little below par, but he was determined to put on a good show for the Spanish supporters. The team were among the favourites and they started their campaign with wins against Morocco, Chile and Honduras 3–0.

Next up were Turkey, who were no match for the Spaniards who completed a routine 3–0 victory. With the game wrapped up, Fábregas was substituted with 30 minutes remaining in order to keep him fresh. The quarter-finals pitted Spain side against Lionel Messi's Argentina, a fixture that should really have been a semi-final or final but the Argentines had finished second in their group and were forced to take a tougher route. It was a big match for Cesc and his team-mates, but they could not find the form that had swept them through the group stage. Argentina were too strong and Messi scored the third in a 3–1 win. The Argentines went on to lift the trophy, triumphing over Nigeria in the final.

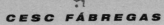
Fábregas had World Cups under his belt now at Under-17 and Under-20 level, so the next natural step for the young midfield star was to feature for the senior squad at a major tournament. The 2006 World Cup was fast approaching, but Euro 2008 looked like the more realistic target, if Cesc could maintain his exciting form. As the Spaniard headed off for a few weeks of rest, he hoped his performances meant he would have an even bigger role to play when the new Premiership season kicked off in August.

7

Cesc Fábregas was thrust further into the spotlight after the summer dealings at Highbury. Wenger accepted a bid from Juventus for Patrick Vieira and the French midfielder headed to Italy in a £13.75 million move. It sent shockwaves of panic around the club but, for Cesc, it opened the door even further to more first-team games.

Wenger obviously had no doubts over his ability to play a full season in central midfield. Many speculated about which big-name star Arsenal would sign to replace Vieira, but the Gunners boss knew he had no need to dabble in the transfer market because he already had the ideal candidate in his squad. Looking back, Fábregas said, 'I knew it was a big chance for me to show everyone that the boss was not wrong and that I could be there to replace Patrick. He is not scared of giving opportunities. That's why I'm so thankful to Arsène Wenger.'

Elsewhere in the Premiership, Arsenal's rivals were very active in the transfer market. Unsurprisingly, Chelsea again flexed their financial muscles as Mourinho paid in excess of £50 million to add Michael Essien, Shaun Wright-Phillips and Asier Del Horno to an already impressive squad. Manchester United were quieter over the summer and just added goalkeeper Edwin van der Sar and Ji-Sung Park. Liverpool, the European champions, made several signings, including the 6ft 7in striker Peter Crouch.

Having finished second last season, the Gunners were pleased to have avoided the Champions League qualifiers.

Instead, they completed a stress-free pre-season and focused on their first league game, at home to Newcastle. Fábregas lined up alongside Gilberto in the centre of midfield and life became much easier after Jermaine Jenas was sent off in the 32nd minute. There was more space for Cesc to set up crisp passing moves but the goals would not come. Wenger substituted him with just under 20 minutes to go and the youngster watched nervously as his team-mates laid siege to the Newcastle goal. Henry finally broke the deadlock from the penalty spot and then van Persie made sure of the three points. Fábregas knew the Gunners would see plenty more sides coming to Highbury with the same mentality as Newcastle, playing one man up front, five in midfield and defending in numbers. It was something he would have to learn to cope with.

Next for Arsenal was a tough assignment away to the champions, Chelsea. Mourinho's side had had the better of their battles the previous season and Fábregas was eager to prove things would be different this time round. But it was the Blues who had the last laugh, winning 1–0 thanks to a Didier Drogba goal. The next few weeks brought more erratic form and questions were asked of Wenger's decision to sell Vieira. Arsenal could be brilliant one week and then feeble the next and it was having a damaging effect on their title chances. They had one of their good days at home to Fulham, winning 4–1 in a match that saw Fábregas play the full 90 minutes for the first time that season.

But the Gunners went from sublime to ridiculous two weeks later. Wenger opted to leave Fábregas on the bench for the trip to Middlesbrough and the Spaniard could only watch as his team-mates surrendered in feeble fashion to the home side. After Maccarone put Boro 2–0 up, Fábregas was sent on to try to rescue something from the match. Reyes scored in the final moments, but it was too little too late.

The start of the Champions League schedule came as a welcome distraction. The campaign began at home to FC Thun and the three points should have been a formality. Fábregas was back in the starting line-up, but the Gunners still struggled to make a breakthrough. Gilberto eventually opened the scoring after half-time, only for FC Thun to equalise within two minutes. Bergkamp replaced Fábregas and the Dutchman finally settled the contest in the final seconds.

Victory over Everton was followed by a goalless draw at West Ham, and Arsenal were already in danger of losing touch with the title contenders but there was some consolation when they shrugged of a history of poor European away form to beat Dutch masters Ajax 2–1. Six points out of six was an excellent start and the Gunners seemed on course to wipe out the memory of last season's early exit at the hands of Bayern Munich.

A 1–0 win over Birmingham kept up the momentum, but a 2–1 defeat at West Brom provided Fábregas and his team-mates with another disappointing away day. They then went on an unbeaten run in all competitions that stretched into December. It began in the Czech Republic where Sparta Prague were beaten 2–0 and that was followed by a 1–0 win against Manchester City at Highbury.

Cesc was rested as Arsenal eased through a Carling Cup-tie with Sunderland but was restored for the derby with Spurs. Tottenham led at half-time and Fábregas and his team-mates needed an error from the Spurs goalkeeper Paul Robinson to snatch an equaliser with less than 15 minutes remaining.

Fábregas had been thrown in at the deep end and had adjusted superbly, especially considering he was still just 18 years of age. It was a tough ask for him to step into a team with so many respected figures and play with confidence. As a result, he sometimes deferred to his more illustrious team-mates at times when he could have delivered the key pass or taken the shot himself. But whenever Bergkamp or Henry called for the ball, he sent it through.

After a 3–0 win over Sparta Prague Arsenal took their place in the second round of the Champions Leage. They also dispatched Sunderland and Wigan in the Premiership, and then Blackburn when Fábregas played a key role, scoring the opening goal with a well-placed shot. It was fitting that, on the day that the football world mourned the death of the legendary George Best, Cesc and Henry put on a master-class worthy of the great legend.

After Arsenal's Carling Cup side had disposed of Championship leaders Reading, the first-team players saw their good run come to end against their nemesis Bolton. Two first-half goals for the Trotters put the game beyond the Gunners and Fábregas was substituted with 20 minutes left. It had been a difficult afternoon for him as Bolton denied him time and space and made good use of the long ball, unsettling the Arsenal defence. A forgettable few weeks followed, and the wear and tear of the season began to show on the young Spanish star.

He made a half-hour cameo in a goalless draw against Ajax in the Champions League but once again the bread and butter business of the league saw Arsenal labour to a 1–0 defeat at Newcastle. Fábregas was constantly harried by a handful of eager Magpie defenders and found his influence restricted. Consequently, the Gunners never got going. Meanwhile Chelsea were in unstoppable form. Mourinho's side had mastered the art of consistency and managed to grind out victories even when not at their best. John Terry and Frank Lampard flourished under Mourinho's management. On form, the Gunners were unstoppable, but when they struggled, points invariably were dropped. But there was a chance to redeem themselves just around the corner.

8

Chelsea were the next visitors to Highbury just before Christmas. While a victory was unlikely to revive Arsenal's title bid, Fábregas was desperate to prove a point to the Blues and restore some pride to his club. Unfortunately, the Gunners' woes continued as Mourinho's side strolled into north London and thoroughly deserved their 2–0 win. The Premiership table made horrific viewing for Gunners fans. Chelsea were 20 points ahead of Arsenal, who had one game in hand. The media wasted no time in mentioning the fact that not long ago Wenger's side had been dubbed the 'Invincibles'. There was even a doubt if they would finish high enough to claim a Champions League spot next season.

Manchester United had also found it impossible to keep up with Chelsea. While they were not as far adrift as Arsenal, Ferguson's side needed a miracle to overtake Mourinho's rampant squad. Strangely, United's clash with Arsenal at Highbury at the start of the New Year was missing some of its usual bite. Perhaps the absences of Roy Keane, who left United in late 2005, and Vieira also played a part.

A weary Fábregas lasted 80 minutes of another goalless draw and was involved in one of the game's key moments as he fell in the area after Gary Neville's sliding tackle. The England defender appeared to take man and ball, but referee Graham Poll waved away the penalty claims. Replays suggested the Spaniard might have had good reason to feel aggrieved. The result not only left Chelsea fans rejoicing but Tottenham's supporters watched in delight as the Gunners dropped yet more points in the race for fourth place.

But on 14 January football fans all over the country were reminded of how good Fábregas and company could be as Arsenal thrashed Middlesbrough 7–0 at Highbury. It was an incredible match, which raised questions of why the Gunners did not produce the same level of clinical finishing on a more regular basis. Thierry Henry scored a hat-trick as the home fans were treated to a master-class in slick, attacking football. But just a week later, a 1–0 loss at Everton underlined the reason why Arsenal were trailing the other top clubs. Fábregas toiled in midfield and found himself frequently frustrated by tenacious Everton challenges. It all boiled over in the closing moments with Tim Cahill and Henry squaring up. Cesc rushed over and threw himself at the Everton midfielder, leaving referee Alan Wiley with no choice but to produce a red card. Fábregas now faced a three-match suspension.

Arsenal went out of the Carling Cup to Wigan and their FA Cup hopes floundered at Bolton. But at least Fábregas was called up to the Spanish senior squad for the first time for the friendly against the Ivory Coast. It was a well-deserved opportunity for the youngster. He told *Marca* newspaper: 'It is a very special day for me because it is the first time that I am joining up with the squad. If I am lucky enough to make my debut, it will be very exciting.'. There was still time for him to compete for a place in the Spanish World Cup squad. Typically understated, the youngster told the press: 'I can only say that I am very happy. I am going to give it everything.'

It was little surprise that Cesc's return from suspension coincided with Arsenal's improved form. The team had lacked

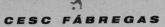
his calm presence in midfield and his ability to spot the right pass at the right time. Goals from Adebayor and Henry sealed a 2–0 victory away to Birmingham as the Gunners tried to build some momentum ahead of the Champions League second round. But the draw had not been kind to them because they were paired with Spanish giants Real Madrid.

9

Despite some negative media coverage, the Gunners travelled to Madrid in high spirits. The Champions League was the only trophy left and they were determined to fight for it. This meant putting recent results to one side and focusing on the 180 minutes ahead. Their opponents boasted 'galacticos' such as Ronaldo, David Beckham, Zinedine Zidane, Roberto Carlos and Raúl, but Arsenal had stars of their own, and Fábregas was one of them.

Most neutrals gave Arsenal little chance of getting a result away from home, but it turned out to be a sensational night for the Gunners; a night that pulled the team closer together; a night that convinced Fábregas once and for all that he belonged on the biggest stage. Partnering Gilberto in central midfield, the Spaniard gave an assured performance as Arsenal achieved the unthinkable. They won.

After a goalless first half, in which the Gunners always looked dangerous, Fábregas came out positively for the second period, knowing that Madrid were there for the taking. The Spanish side appeared shaky in defence and Wenger urged his players to be positive. Henry produced the perfect response, gliding past several Real challenges before slotting the ball past goalkeeper Iker Casillas. The Bernabeu was stunned into silence. Strong defending and plenty of energetic midfield work helped the Gunners protect their lead and Fábregas even had the audacity to employ a Cruyff turn to outwit his marker near the halfway line late in the game as he turned on the style. When he was substituted in the dying moments, the Spaniard received a great ovation from all sections of the crowd. It was a massive moment in Arsenal's season.

The critics were generous: Amy Lawrence of the *Guardian* explained: 'In his [Fábregas'] first match as a professional footballer in his homeland he had earned the instant respect of his compatriots.' The Madrid-based *AS* praised the Arsenal scouts who had tempted Cesc away from Barça, while the Barcelona media mocked Real's incompetent display and took pride in the fact that Cesc had been educated at their cantera. Lawrence also pointed out the irony of the Catalan coverage. She wrote: 'Local pride in Fábregas' development is one thing, but it is a sore point for Barcelona that he left to make the grade. The story exposes how difficult it is to balance developing youngsters with signing experienced players. Fábregas has already played almost 100 games for Arsenal and he appreciates the equality he enjoyed at Highbury from day one, saying: "I never trained with the first team at Barcelona. It's not like that here [at Arsenal]. Here you're treated like all the other players."'

The Madrid game had taken a physical and emotional toll on Arsenal and it showed at Blackburn at the weekend because Arsenal failed to match Rovers' intensity and lost 1–0. There was barely time for Fábregas to take in the defeat before he headed to Valladolid for one of the biggest occasions of his career to date. Ever since he had heard the news of his call-up to the Spanish senior squad, he had been looking forward to the country's friendly against the Ivory Coast. Even though it was the youngster's first call-up, manager Luis Aragones had no doubts about throwing him into the fray, picking Fábregas in a four-man midfield. He became the second youngest player in Spain's history to represent the national team.

He also contributed to the team's opening goal, scored by David Villa, and was one of the success stories on the night for Spain. The media raved about his performance. He told the press: 'I am happy with how it all went and, even better, we won. It's one of the happiest days of my life. I played well and the crowd and coach helped me a lot. It was a busy week, but very special.'

Back in the Premiership, Arsenal produced a more fluent, confident display against Fulham. With one eye on the second leg of their Champions League fixture against Real Madrid in midweek, Wenger left Fábregas on the bench, but the youngster came on for the final 10 minutes and scored the team's fourth goal in a 4–0 victory.

With David Beckham returning to play in England for the first time since his move to Madrid in 2003, all eyes were on Highbury. Again Real sent out a team packed with international stars and again Arsenal held firm. Lehmann was forced to make several vital stops, but for the most part Fábregas and his team-mates kept the visitors at bay. It should have been a nervy time for Cesc, considering his age and the knife-edge nature of the contest, but he got on with his job with the minimum of fuss. The only sign of any nerves came when he missed a decent first-half chance. Showing the commitment that had been missing too often in Premiership outings, Arsenal defended and Real could not break through. They did it. They knocked out the great Real Madrid.

Cesc's individual performances across the two legs in front of hordes of Spanish viewers back home, enhanced his chances of snatching a place in the Spanish World Cup squad. The target had become a realistic one. If he kept playing this well, Aragones would be mad not to pick the youngster. After witnessing his brilliance and maturity against Real, there was no doubt the Spanish public would be calling for Fábregas to go to Germany.

But before that he and Arsenal were drawn against Fabio Capello's Juventus in the first leg of their Champions League quarter-final. Now everyone would see how much the Gunners were really missing Vieira.

10

Fábregas chose this night to produce one of his best-ever displays, working hard to win possession and distributing the ball confidently. His big moment came just before half-time. Pires made a brilliant challenge on Vieira, Henry collected the loose ball and found Cesc. The Spaniard worked an opening against French international Lilian Thuram and drilled the ball past goalkeeper Gianluigi Buffon into the bottom corner. The ground erupted. Vieira gingerly got to his feet as the crowd jeered. After all the comments about the Frenchman's summer exit, it was symbolic that he was the man who had been dispossessed in the build-up to the goal. Out with the old...

Fábregas was involved in another slick move in the second half as Arsenal looked to kill off their opponents. He was not tracked by the Juventus midfield and found himself through on goal. He shaped to shoot, only to lay the ball across towards Henry. The pass was a little behind the French striker, but with Buffon stranded by Cesc's disguised ball, Henry rolled it into the net. 2–0. The Italians were rattled. Vieira was booked and then two Juventus players were sent off in the final few minutes. At the final whistle, Fábregas basked in the glory of the moment. He had been sensational at the heart of everything the Gunners had done. Suddenly the headlines focused on the 'new generation' at Arsenal and how far they could go in the competition. Vieira and Juventus had been slow and laboured; the Gunners displayed a youthful swagger.

Post-match, all the talk surrounded the diminutive Spaniard. Henry told the media: 'Cesc is doing extremely well. If you let him play he can kill a team. I think you see more of him when we play five in the middle. He knew today that he had Gilberto behind him. He knows when to go into the box, when to join and when he had time on the ball.'

The return match did not live up to the first. Though Wenger sent out a defensive line-up, the Gunners always looked dangerous with the passing range of Fábregas and the pace of Henry and Arsenal went through. Their semi-final opponents? Spanish side Villarreal.

Considering the emotional roller-coaster ride of the past few weeks, it was hardly surprising that the Gunners could not lift themselves away to a resurgent Manchester United, who were attempting to put pressure on Chelsea. Arsenal gave it their all, but their weary legs just could not compete with the home side who won 2–0.

A few matches later and Arsenal were in serious danger of missing out on fourth place and Fábregas' didn't look like being fit enough to face Villarreal. But at least he knew who the Gunners boss had voted for in the PFA Player and Young Player of the Year awards: 'My list is very short. It is Thierry Henry and Cesc Fábregas, and by miles. You cannot see anyone coming close to them.' And in the end Fábregas was fit enough to start the game.

The first leg was at Highbury and Cesc urged the home fans to make it an intimidating arena for the visitors, who were strangers to this stage of European football. With a five-man midfield, Arsenal always looked dangerous with the passing range of Fábregas and the pace of Henry. The Gunners put Villarreal on the back foot and finally took advantage just before half-time as Kolo Toure scrambled the ball home. The visitors, though, did not crumble. Fábregas, playing through the pain, helped create several good opportunities, but their opponents also forced Lehmann into some smart stops. In the end, Arsenal had to settle for a 1–0 victory.

After a volatile draw against Tottenham, attention immediately turned to the return match in Spain. It was not really Fábregas' type of match, as he and his team-mates spent much of the game scrapping for possession and breaking up attacks. But the youngster gave his all in midfield, supporting the tireless Gilberto and helping to relieve the tension with careful passing. This match was all about stamina and desire – attractive football went out of the window.

On the night, the Gunners had reason to be eternally thankful to Lehmann, who kept up his fine run of form. Real Madrid and Juventus had not found a way past him and nor could Villarreal. But with Arsenal clinging on desperately and with only seconds to go, their worst nightmare happened. Full-back Gael Clichy challenged Villarreal forward Jose Mari and referee Ivan Ivanov stunned the Gunners by awarding a penalty. After all the hard graft, a dubious decision by an official had given the Spaniards a last-gasp chance to get out of jail.

Argentine Juan Roman Riquelme, Villarreal's star man, took the penalty, but Lehmann produced one last heroic contribution, guessing the right way sending the Gunners to Paris for the Champions League final. Fábregas was overcome with emotion. It may not have been his finest performance for the club, but it had been one of the most rewarding and memorable. The following evening, Barcelona narrowly held off the challenge of AC Milan to book their place in the final. Cesc would be facing his childhood team in the biggest game of his career. It made the occasion even more special.

As the pursuit of fourth place entered the crucial final stages, Wenger did not dare rest his big-name players. So just days after the momentous night in Spain, Fábregas was back in action away to Sunderland. Wenger was relieved to see his side wrap up the points in the first half, scoring three times and outclassing their feeble opponents, who were heading back to the Championship with a record low points total. Fábregas grabbed the Gunners' second goal, benefiting from Henry's powerful run.

Tottenham were showing signs of faltering and Arsenal were ready and waiting. A 3–1 victory at Manchester City on 4 May cranked up the pressure another notch. Spurs' lead had been cut to just one point going into the final weekend of the Premiership season. Fábregas and company just had to better Tottenham's result.

It set up a mouth-watering finale for Arsenal's very last game at Highbury. Nobody could have scripted it better. Fábregas and his team-mates had given the old stadium a terrific European run and now the squad prepared to finish on a high. Wigan were their opponents while Tottenham faced West Ham.

11

With a 10-day break between the crucial Wigan fixture and the Champions League final, Wenger did not worry about resting his players. He selected a full-strength side and, although the visitors did their best to spoil the party, going 2–1 up after 30 minutes, it was Arsenal's day. The noise from around the ground, especially the North Bank, was incredible as news filtered through that West Ham had beaten Tottenham, who had suffered as food poisoning swept through the squad. Arsenal had snatched fourth place and all eyes turned to Paris.

Barcelona boasted a star-studded side, including Fábregas' cantera colleague Messi, Samuel Eto'o and the great Brazilian Ronaldinho. But Wenger hoped the Catalan giants were just as wary of the talent of Fábregas, Henry and Pires. And Cesc was confident. He said, 'Barcelona are beatable. Yes, they are a great team – they have shown that over the last two years – and it is going to be difficult. But it has been like that all through the competition. Against Madrid we were not the favourites and against Juventus we were not the favourites. And I hope it will continue.'

Arsenal continued with the 4-5-1 formation that had helped the team reach the final. Walking out and feeling the atmosphere inside the stadium, even just for the warm-up, was an incredible sensation for Fábregas and he soaked up every minute of it. This was the type of match he was born to play in.

However, after all the ecstasy of the occasion, the anthems and the team photo, Arsenal suffered a cruel blow in the 18th minute of the game when Lehmann was red-carded for bringing down Eto'o just outside the area. It was a disastrous moment after what had been a promising start from the Gunners. Pires was sacrificed as Manuel Almunia took over in goal. From then on it was always going to be an uphill struggle for Fábregas and his team-mates. But the Gunners dug deep and fought for their lives. Fábregas got through a mountain of work in midfield, denying the likes of Ronaldinho and Messi the freedom to punish Arsenal. Then, to everyone's surprise, the 10 men took the lead. Emmanuel Eboué won a free-kick on the right and Henry's delivery was powered home by Campbell, who was only back in the side due to an injury to Senderos. Could Cesc and company pull this off?

Wenger urged his team to stay focused. As the rain fell, the Gunners began to sense this might be their night and the game became increasingly scrappy. Barcelona threw men forward in search of an equaliser and a weary Henry came close to punishing them. A second goal would have clinched the game. Wenger decided to bring on Flamini to replace Fábregas for the final 15 minutes, feeling that the Spaniard had given everything to the cause and thinking that fresh legs might make the difference in defending the slender lead. Instead, Barcelona made the breakthrough. The youngster was devastated as he sat helplessly on the bench, watching the trophy slipping out of the team's hands.

Worse was to follow. Juliano Belletti burst forward and broke Arsenal hearts. His shot nestled in the net and Barça breathed a huge sigh of relief as they celebrated a dramatic turnaround with two goals in four minutes. The Gunners had been floored. Barcelona hung on to win 2–1 and Cesc was distraught.

The Arsenal players were very bitter after the game, feeling robbed and cheated by the officials. Fábregas told the press: 'You have to be fair in football – you have to be honest and "well done" to you if you've won, but you have to win in a good way. I don't like to be in the position of saying things about the referee, but maybe it's true. If you look at the first goal for Barça, it's clearly offside.' Cesc was also furious at the treatment received by Henry from defenders Rafael Marquez and Carlos Puyol.

For Cesc, though, the season was not over. He had to put the disappointments of the domestic campaign behind him and focus on the next challenge, because Aragones and Spain would be relying on him. The European adventure was about to go global.

12

Fábregas had made no secret of his desire to represent his country on the biggest stage, saying, 'The World Cup is a dream for me. It is the greatest recognition a footballer can have and it would be incredible to be in Germany with the squad.' But he could understand why he might miss out because, 'The truth is I am very young and I know that there is difficulty because there is a lot of talent. I have my feet on the ground.' However, with his seat on the plane to Germany confirmed, Fábregas could look forward to an exciting summer with his international colleagues.

Spain had made hard work of reaching the tournament. Although they didn't lose a match in their qualifying campaign, they drew five of their 10 matches and allowed Serbia & Montenegro to top the group by two points. This forced the Spaniards into a high-stakes play-off against Slovakia, which they won comfortably. Their performances in Germany would have to be better.

Spain, like most nations, played a string of warm-up matches prior to the tournament. Cesc was eager to perform well and make a good impression on the manager but there was strong competition for places in midfield and in fact he found himself on the bench for their first match against Ukraine in Leipzig, after Aragones opted for Xavi, Xabi Alonso and Marcos Senna ahead of Fábregas. But with 13 minutes to go Cesc was sent on, becoming his country's youngest-ever World Cup player at just 19 years and 41 days old.

Cesc wasted no time in telling the media that the team had the perfect balance: 'Every team has their tricks: there are sides that are stronger, but less technically gifted or the reverse, but I believe that Spain has a very good mix.'

Spain's next match was against Tunisia in Stuttgart. As expected, the team stayed unchanged but made a nightmare start, falling behind after eight minutes. Aragones was far from amused and made two changes at half time: Luis Garcia was replaced by Raul and Marcos Senna made way for Fábregas. Cesc was determined to make the most of this chance and he, more than anyone, helped turn the match around.

Gradually, Tunisia began to tire and Fábregas stamped his authority on the game. Spain's equaliser came after 72 minutes. Cesc has never been shy to try his luck with long-range shots and it paid dividends on this occasion. His strike was fumbled by the Tunisian goalkeeper and Raul netted the rebound. Fábregas was not finished yet though. Four minutes later, his pinpoint pass behind the Tunisia defence released Torres, who comfortably made it 2–1. The game had been turned on its head. Torres added a third from the penalty spot late on, but there was no doubt Fábregas had been the catalyst for the win.

Fábregas' display had pleased all those who saw it, including the great Argentine playmaker Diego Maradona, who told Spanish television station Cuatro: 'Cesc gave Spain the final ball it was lacking in the first half.' In a personal address to the Spaniard, Maradona added: 'I hope you carry on playing football like that. It was spectacular.'

The victory put Spain into the second round, taking the pressure off the players for their final group match against Saudi Arabia which they won 1–0. Then came France. The coach decided he wanted more creativity and felt that Cesc was the man for the moment. The Spaniards had not expected to face France in the second round but Switzerland had pipped the French to first place in Group G, setting up a mouth-watering second-round clash between two of Europe's finest teams. Fábregas and company would now have to outwit the likes of Vieira, Zidane and Henry to reach the quarter-finals. It was the tie of the round and everyone was looking forward to it. Writing for the *Independent*, Gerry Francis said, 'For the last few championships I've had a bet on Spain. In Cesc Fábregas, they've got a player who's blossoming, is used to big games and can make the difference.'

But it wasn't to be a memorable night for the Spaniards. Fábregas and his team-mates never really settled into their rhythm, even though they found themselves leading just before the half-hour mark when Lilian Thuram was adjudged to have fouled Pablo Ibanez in the penalty area. Villa converted the spot-kick. The joy was short-lived. Franck Ribery equalised before half-time and the French looked the superior side as Zidane rolled back the years with some vintage touches.

The crucial moments came late on as Henry won a free-kick for a challenge by Barcelona defender Carlos Puyol, who was renewing his duel with the striker from the Champions League final, and the resulting delivery allowed Vieira to put France ahead. Just seven minutes remained. It was a crushing blow and left Fábregas and company little time to respond. They were shell-shocked as their world came crashing down around them. As Spain pushed forward desperately for a dramatic equaliser, the French put the game to bed. Zidane capped an excellent individual display by scoring a composed third on the break.

The dream was over.

Fábregas told the Spanish press how the agony of the defeat had left him with 'a bad taste in his mouth'. He explained: 'Elimination is hard to take. We have had a good tournament and we are leaving much earlier than anticipated. We had many expectations and to be heading home early makes it a little difficult.' The players watched the match at home on TV and saw Italy beat France and Zidane's extra-time head-butt on Marco Materazzi.

13

Cesc's performances in Germany had particularly caught the attention of Real Madrid and he jumped to the top of their transfer wish list. It was easy to see why. With all the 'galacticos' in the Madrid squad, a calm, measured passer would help to get the best out of the likes of Raul and Ronaldo. Reports flew in from all directions, everyone claiming to know the latest situation. In late June, Ramón Calderón, a candidate in the Real Madrid presidential elections, claimed he had agreed a deal to bring Fábregas to the Bernabeu if he was elected. It was a worrying time for the Arsenal fans as reports maintained that the Spaniard would be leaving the club. Pedja Mijatovic, the Sporting Director of Calderón's campaign, told the media that 'Cesc and Kaka [of AC Milan] will play for Real Madrid' and it did plenty to unsettle Wenger as the Frenchman planned for the new season.

But Fábregas was happy at Arsenal, because they were now playing at the Emirates Stadium. The increased capacity – from 38,000 to 60,000 – meant that the atmosphere inside the stadium would be incredible. The other big news was that Thierry Henry was staying at Arsenal and wouldn't be joining Barcelona.

Meanwhile Arsenal's title challengers looked hungry. Chelsea's two-year league domination showed no signs of ending, especially with the additions of German midfielder Michael Ballack and Ukrainian front man Andriy Shevchenko. By contrast, Manchester United had been fairly restrained. Michael Carrick was their only major purchase, costing £18.6 million, but Sir Alex Ferguson was delighted to welcome Paul Scholes back from a troublesome eye injury. Liverpool had also rebuilt over the summer in a desperate attempt to bring the title back to Merseyside. Fábregas knew it would be a tough ask for the Gunners to fight off such strong competition, but he remained confident about the team's ability. The big question was whether the Arsenal side could find consistency on their travels.

But before Arsenal could focus on their league campaign, they had a Champions League qualifier against Dinamo Zagreb. In the first leg, in Croatia, Cesc was the star of the show. Arsenal failed to break through in the opening period, but Fábregas came to life in the final half hour, opening the scoring with a well-placed shot. Van Persie doubled the lead a minute later before Cesc found the net again, outwitting several defenders and giving the Gunners a comfortable three-goal cushion for the return leg.

This was followed by their first league game at the Emirates. Aston Villa, appeared to relish their role as party poopers in front of a crowd of 60,023. Arsenal needed a late equaliser from Gilberto Silva to rescue a point after Olof Mellberg had headed the visitors in front.

An opportunity quickly arrived for the team to make amends. In midweek, the Gunners completed a 5–1 aggregate victory over Dinamo Zagreb and booked their place in the Champions League group stage.

Back in the Premiership, the Gunners' wobble continued away to Manchester City. They were finding goals hard to come by, despite creating a hatful of chances. Arsenal dominated the first half at Eastlands but found the path to goal blocked and returned to London nursing a 1–0 defeat. Fábregas had not played badly, but Wenger wanted to see the Spaniard getting into goal-scoring positions more often.

Arsenal finally brought an end to the on-running Ashley Cole saga as they narrowly beat the transfer deadline to secure a swap deal that brought French defender William Gallas to the Emirates and a cheque for £5 million.

Fábregas soon headed back to his homeland for the international break as Spain began their qualifying campaign against Liechtenstein in Badajoz, winning 4–0. He was picked in the starting line-up and played 63 minutes before he was replaced by Iniesta. By this time Spain were 3–0 up and cruising to victory. Four days later, away to Northern Ireland, things were not quite so rosy. Fábregas started on the bench but was soon sent on after David Albelda limped off through injury. This, though, was a humbling night for the Spanish as a David Healy hat-trick condemned the visitors to a 3–2 defeat.

Fábregas was still stunned by the result when he arrived back in north London. The international break did little to improve Arsenal's fortunes in the Premiership. A second home league fixture brought another draw as frustration mounted at the Emirates. Meanwhile, Manchester United had collected 12 points out of 12 and were top of the Premiership; Arsenal had two points from their three games.

It had not taken Fábregas long to understand the intensity of the rivalry between the two clubs and he was desperate to put one over on United in their next match. It was an eventful contest, in which Arsenal kept the United big guns quiet. Rooney contributed little up front for the home side, while Ronaldo struggled to make his usual impact. The Gunners won a first-half penalty when keeper Tomas Kuszczak, fouled Emmanuel Adebayor. Gilberto Silva stepped up to the spot but, to Fábregas' dismay, Kuszczak saved.

As United became increasingly frustrated, Fábregas drove his side forward. With just four minutes remaining, the

Gunners found the knockout blow, thanks largely to Fábregas' vision. The youngster chased and harried Ronaldo into a mistake in his own half and seized on the loose ball. He dribbled goalwards before sliding a clever ball through to Adebayor, who placed the ball under Kuszczak and into the net. The away end of the ground went wild.

Having beaten United without Henry, confidence was high again around the Emirates. The Frenchman returned to the side for the visit of Sheffield United and the Gunners completed a 3–0 victory, with all the goals coming in the final 25 minutes. Despite suffering a cut lip during the game, Fábregas produced some sublime moments, including the assist for Gallas to give Arsenal the lead. The Emirates 'jinx' had been lifted; the Gunners had won in the league at home.

A midweek clash with Porto saw Arsenal keep another clean sheet on the way to a solid 2–0 victory. Maximum points so far in Europe represented an excellent start and a buoyant Arsenal grabbed a fifth-consecutive win at the weekend away at Charlton.

The international break saw Fábregas meet up with his international colleagues for two fixtures, first a Euro 2008 qualifier against Sweden and then a friendly with Argentina. After the defeat to Northern Ireland in their last qualifier, the Spaniards needed a positive response against the Swedes to stamp their authority on the group. Fábregas received another starting role as Aragones continued to show faith in the youngster. This, though, was a game to forget for Fábregas both on a personal and team level. Sweden won 2–0 and dominated the contest, scoring in the first and last 10 minutes. That made two losses from three games, and just three points out of a possible nine.

After a below par display, Fábregas was named among the substitutes for the friendly with Argentina and only entered the action for the final 15 minutes. David Villa's second-half

penalty proved decisive as Spain claimed an impressive 2–1 win that gave the morale in the camp a little boost.

Back in domestic action, the Gunners' run of victories stretched to six against Watford at the Emirates. Cesc and his colleagues were putting their slow start behind them and moving up the table. But a defeat away to CSKA Moscow in the Champions League ended Arsenal's hot streak. In the freezing temperatures of the Russian capital, the Gunners succumbed 1–0 against skilful opponents and surrendered their 100 percent record in Group G.

Above: Fábregas takes the silver cup for Spain Under 17s, beaten 1–0 by Brazil in the 2003 World Championship.

Left: A jubilant Fábregas celebrates scoring the fifth goal against Wolverhampton Wanderers in the fourth round of the 2003 Carling Cup.

Expectations are high for the fresh-faced Fábregas, here shown at a press conference on the eve of Arsenal's Champions League match against Real Madrid.

Left: Bergkamp chases Fábregas during a practice session at the club's training ground in North London.

Below: Fábregas battles for the ball with Barcelona's Mark van Bommel during the UEFA Champions League final in May 2006.

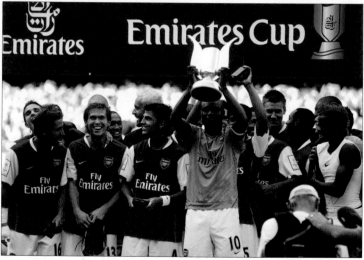

Above: Fábregas vies with Vieira as Spain play France in the 2006 World Cup.

Below: Arsenal celebrate their 2007 triumph over Inter Milan, lifting the Emirates trophy high in the air.

Fábregas signing.

Above: Banter at an international training session in autumn 2007.

Below: Fábregas scores a stunning opener against AC Milan in the Champions League in 2008.

Fábregas gets a pep talk from Wenger during training.

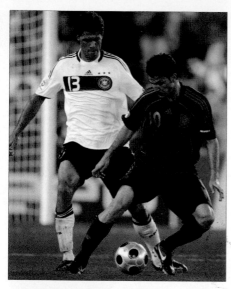

Left: Fábregas takes control during the Euro 2008 final.

Below: Keeping the ball away from Roy Keane in August 2004.

14

In mid-October Arsenal showed their faith in Fábregas by offering him a new eight-year contract to keep at the club until 2014. Cesc wasted no time in expressing his delight at agreeing terms, telling the Arsenal club website: 'I am so happy here. I wanted to pay back the club, especially Arsène Wenger for the support and faith he has shown in me. What is important now is for the team to realise its potential and win trophies. That is our main aim, that is my aim as well.' He should have added, and we all want to be consistent.

Arsenal defeated Reading 4–0 but then started dropping silly points and they became too easily rattled on their travels. It was simply was not good enough. And Fábregas was becoming increasingly frustrated with the way his team-mates were being criticised by the media and with the fact that everyone was so keen to draw direct comparisons with the past. He made his feelings clear on several occasions, including during this interview with the *Independent*: 'You cannot say, "Oh, Diaby the new Vieira, Adebayor the new Kanu, Theo Walcott the new Henry." Maybe they will [be] in the future, but you cannot tell them now they will be the next guys.'

A win over Liverpool emphasised how Arsenal could raise their game for the big matches but fail against the league's weaker teams, including Newcastle with whom they had a frustrating draw. Yet again, a visiting team had come to the Emirates and taken the lead but though Henry equalised with

20 minutes to go, the Gunners couldn't find the winning goal. Fábregas had several chances but failed to make the most of them. The mood was improved in midweek, though, when Arsenal beat Hamburg 3–1 in the Champions League to go top of Group G, with Cesc creating countless openings for his team-mates. At least things were falling into place in Europe.

Then came two soul-destroying defeats in the space of four days, and Arsenal's season hit the rocks as their away-day woes came back to haunt them. First, they were soundly beaten 3–1 by Bolton and then they were beaten 2–1 away to Fulham.

With Henry facing a spell on the sidelines, the north London derby against Tottenham could not have come at a worse time. Fábregas, though, remained upbeat and the side put in their best performance for several weeks, with Adebayor opening the scoring and Gilberto converting two penalties, one in each half, sealing a 3–0 victory. Fábregas again pushed forward into good positions, but the goals just would not come for him.

The Gunners then travelled to Portugal in midweek for an important tie with Porto, and the 0–0 draw put them into the second round. Next up? Chelsea at Stamford Bridge.

The travelling fans predictably jeered Ashley Cole at every opportunity and their team matched the Blues stride for stride. Fábregas had to make a goal-line clearance in the first half to keep the game goalless and Chelsea became increasingly frustrated as the Gunners harried, chased and forced the champions into mistakes. After some comedy theatrics from Jens Lehmann and Didier Drogba, Arsenal grew in confidence and shocked Stamford Bridge by taking the lead with just 12 minutes to go. Flamini played a neat one-two with Hleb and his shot beat Petr Cech. To Fábregas' dismay, the Blues fought back and equalised through a stunning Michael Essien strike. It was the only way Chelsea were going to get past the Arsenal rearguard – a sensational hit with the outside of the boot.

15

For all the improvements Arsenal had shown in their away games, the team continued to drop points at the Emirates. It was a reversal of the previous campaign when their struggles came on the road. The latest visiting side to leave with a share of the spoils was Portsmouth, who gained a 2–2 draw and might have had more after going 2–0 up. Fábregas forced Pompey keeper David James into one good save and was a driving force as Arsenal clawed their way back to parity.

Two days before Christmas, the Gunners finally hit top form at the Emirates, hammering Blackburn 6–2. It was a masterclass in attacking football and, although three goals in the final five minutes gave the score-line a flattering look, Wenger was delighted with his forwards. Fábregas thoroughly enjoyed the occasion but despite numerous opportunities to score just was not clinical enough and luck seemed to be against him. The bottom line, however, was that Cesc had not scored for Arsenal since August.

The festive period was bringing out the best in the Gunners. A 2–1 win at Watford on Boxing Day kept the momentum going, with van Persie scoring the winner with seven minutes left. Fábregas looked a little weary at times, but sparked into life as the team chased the decisive goal. The three points saw Arsenal move into third place, handing them an advantage over Liverpool, Bolton and Portsmouth, who were all fighting with the Gunners for a Champions League berth. But a trip to Sheffield United was a reminder of the flaws in the Arsenal squad as they were out-muscled by the Premiership newcomers and lost 1–0. Cesc began the match on the bench as Wenger opted to ring the changes, a move that backfired badly. Fábregas was introduced after 64 minutes, but the damage had been done and even the Spaniard could not turn things around, despite midfielder Phil Jagielka being called into emergency service in goal for the Blades.

Fábregas and his team-mates began 2007 in style with a 4–0 home win over Charlton. Van Persie scored twice and Arsenal were sparked by the return to fitness of Thierry Henry. Cesc's link-up play was typically precise and his shot led to the penalty that saw Charlton defender Osei Sankofa sent off after just 29 minutes. Henry opened the scoring from the spot. Special mention should also go to Justin Hoyte, who grabbed the team's second goal. As Jim van Wijk of *PA Sport* observed, it was the first time since September 2005 that an English player in an Arsenal shirt had found the net in the Premiership - an incredible statistic.

Arsene Wenger made one significant move during the January transfer window, completing a loan deal that sent Jose Antonio Reyes to Real Madrid until the end of the season in exchange for Brazilian Julio Baptista.

Suspension kept Fábregas out of the FA Cup third-round clash with Liverpool at Anfield when Tomas Rosicky scored two fine goals to put his side on the way to a 3–1 victory. The two teams met again in midweek, this time in the Carling Cup quarter-final. Both managers opted to select a blend of first-team stars, fringe players and youngsters, but it was Wenger's team that produced the vastly superior performance. Fábregas was one of the big names in the side and, with fellow regulars Toure and Adebayor, he gave a flawless display. New boy Julio Baptista was the hero despite missing a penalty. He bagged four goals in a thrilling contest, which ended 6–3.

The run continued as January turned out to be the best month so far for Wenger's squad. Arsenal won 2–0 at Ewood Park and then came a home match against Manchester United.

Fábregas found life tough in midfield in the first half as Paul Scholes and Michael Carrick dominated possession. The game remained goalless at half-time, but after the break United seized the initiative as Wayne Rooney headed in Patrice Evra's cross.

Wenger had reminded his players to make full use of their youthful energy and they came roaring back into the game. Fábregas became more involved in the build-up play and United began to tire. Then, with seven minutes to go, Cesc made his most important contribution, winning possession and finding Rosicky whose cross was buried by van Persie at the back post.

United were there for the taking. Tiredness was forgotten as adrenalin took over and Arsenal searched for the knockout blow. It came in injury time. Eboue broke free on the right and his cross was inch perfect for Henry to head past van der Sar. It completed a staggering turnaround and presented the Emirates with its most thrilling moment to date.

Suddenly the early season gloom had been lifted. Even the club's youngsters and fringe players picked up on the positive vibe, as they showed in a rousing Carling Cup semi-final first-leg comeback against Tottenham. Cesc was given a rare run-out in the competition, but things did not start well as Spurs took a 2–0 lead. Baptista then scored twice to earn Arsenal a draw and make them favourites. But first it was time for some talk.

After the match he said, 'You could see on Sunday against Manchester United we scored two goals in the last ten minutes. Why not in the second half last night? I think all the teams drop a little bit in the last 20 minutes and it is then that we have to push quickly and be stronger offensively. We are showing everyone that even with the young players you can go far in this competition. You have to congratulate them for what they are doing because it is amazing.' It was funny to hear the Spaniard refer to the 'young players' as if he was not one of them.

The players also had an important team meeting which had played a part in sorting out their inconsistency away from home. Fábregas said, 'We realised that if we didn't change our mentality we would always struggle in those kinds of games. From then on, we've been showing great character, great attitude and doing really well. We had a talk between ourselves and decided that we had to become more competitive.'

But despite that, Arsenal's inability to kill teams off at home haunted them yet again in the FA Cup fourth round against Bolton. Trailing to a Kevin Nolan goal, the Gunners were again indebted to Fábregas for hauling them back into the contest. Then came the second leg against Tottenham in the Carling Cup semi-final. Fábregas started on the bench. It was a scrappy contest and the Arsenal boss sent the midfielder on in the 79th minute, by which time Adebayor had given the Gunners the advantage. Shortly after Cesc's arrival, however, Tottenham equalised through Mido to force extra-time. Wenger must have cursed. He had not wanted Fábregas to clock up a further half hour that night. Fortunately, a strike from the young forward Jeremie Aliadiere and a Pascal Chimbonda own goal settled the semi-final in Arsenal's favour.

International duty called again with Spain due to play England at Old Trafford. The match might only have been a friendly, but both teams were keen to record a victory. Cesc had to make do with a place on the substitutes' bench but he came on for the final 15 minutes, by which time Iniesta had put Spain 1–0 up with a fantastic strike, and they held on for a spirited win.

Back at Arsenal, it was a depressingly familiar story for Fábregas, with opposing sides going ahead on a regular basis. Wigan went 1–0 up in the 35th minute and held on until the closing stages before crumbling to a 2–1 defeat.

After the FA Cup replay win against Bolton they faced Blackburn in three days' time in what turned out to be a very fiery encounter.

16

Arsenal squared off with Blackburn at the Emirates in the fifth round in what turned out to be a frustrating afternoon for Fábregas, and one that boiled over at the final whistle. Blackburn arrived with a game plan to defend in numbers and play physically. Their keeper, Brad Friedel, was in excellent form and the visitors received a couple of generous decisions from the referee. Nonetheless, Fábregas should have acknowledged that Blackburn had fought hard and had earned a replay. Instead, he sulked. Finally his temper got the better of him and he vented his anger on Rovers boss Mark Hughes.

Cesc had worked his socks off in midfield, despite the close attentions of the Blackburn players and was clearly annoyed. Wagging his finger towards Hughes, he demanded to know how, as a former Barcelona player, he could tolerate such a defensive style of play. It looked like rather poor sportsmanship and it was certainly naïve. Did he really expect Rovers to come and play expansive football after losing 6–2 at the Emirates earlier in the season?

Fortunately, Hughes shrugged off the Spaniard's outburst. He said, 'Maybe he was frustrated with the way the game went and how he played as an individual, and that he wasn't able to exert as much influence as he normally does. Maybe now he has calmed down, he has understood what we tried to do.' Cesc later apologised to the Rovers boss and Hughes seemed satisfied when he added, 'He's got a winning mentality and we appreciate that. Let's move on.'

It was only at times like these that people remembered that Fábregas was still only 19 years old, but it clearly emphasised just how badly he wanted to win and just how highly he regarded playing attractive football.

He quickly needed to regain his composure and focus. The Gunners had the next round of the Champions League coming up and they were drawn against PSV Eindhoven of Holland. It would be a tricky tie but Wenger's side were clear favourites. The first leg was in Eindhoven and Arsenal travelled with plenty of belief. Unfortunately, they left that belief in the dressing room on what was a damaging European night. PSV won the match 1–0 and stopped Arsenal from finding their rhythm, though Fábregas went close with a shot from the edge of the penalty area.

Fábregas put the disappointment to one side as Arsenal faced Chelsea at the weekend in the Carling Cup final. True to his word, Wenger kept faith with his fringe players and youngsters, mixing in a few first-team stars. Cesc made the starting line-up alongside fellow young guns Theo Walcott, Armand Traoré and Denilson, against a Chelsea side packed with internationals. Walcott handed Arsenal the perfect start but Drogba soon equalised for the Blues. The drama continued in the second half when Terry was rushed to hospital after swallowing his tongue. It was a stomach-churning moment and left a number of players feeling queasy. Chelsea recovered quickest and Drogba pounced to score the winner with six minutes to go.

Emotions boiled over late on as the Gunners tried in vain to level the scores. A 14-man brawl led to red cards for Arsenal's Toure and Adebayor and John Obi Mikel of Chelsea. Fábregas needlessly got himself involved with Lampard, earning himself a yellow card, and the Spaniard also confronted Drogba and Mourinho as referee Howard Webb struggled to keep control of the players. The unseemly finale to the match spoiled what had otherwise been an intriguing battle. Cesc's temper had again got the better of him and it was something he needed to sort out. Quick.

Looking back at the Carling Cup final, former Gunner Paul Merson wrote in the *Evening Standard*: 'Cesc Fábregas has to learn to calm down if he is ever going to become an Arsenal great. It was very disappointing to see his petulant behaviour against Chelsea and it is becoming a worrying trend. The 19-year-old Spaniard has bags of ability, but it is being undermined by his own temper and his inability to control it. Everyone gets wound up during matches and the midfielder has made a habit of being in the headlines for all the wrong reasons in recent weeks.'

A miserable week for the Gunners was completed with a 1–0 defeat away to Blackburn in their FA Cup fifth-round replay. Rovers came out as if fuelled by Fábregas' outburst 10 days earlier and a late Benni McCarthy goal ended Arsenal's hopes of a domestic cup triumph. With one eye on the Champions League second-leg match against PSV the following week, Wenger chose to rest several players, including Fábregas and Henry, for the trip to Ewood Park and the Gunners paid for that decision.

Cesc was back for the 2–1 home win over Reading but won't recall it fondly because with the game seemingly sealed, he contrived to end his goal-scoring drought by putting the ball into his *own* net from a corner. Having earlier fluffed a simple chance in front of goal, it was an afternoon to forget for the Spaniard.

All eyes were fixed on the Emirates again as PSV arrived for the second leg of their European tie. Even though Fábregas and company were regarded as a stronger outfit, there was plenty of anxiety around the Emirates. A crowd of

60,073 poured through the gates, hoping for an emphatic Arsenal display but fearing a nail-biting night. After a tight first half, Arsenal got the all-important breakthrough just before the hour mark when the Brazilian defender Alex diverted the ball into his own net from a corner. The Gunners were level in the tie.

Fábregas quickly looked to take the game by the scruff of the neck, feeding Adebayor, whose effort was well saved, and then he got into a good position himself, only to blaze over. Henry had been summoned from the bench as Wenger tried in vain to avoid a tense finish. As everyone began to think about the possibility of extra-time, the unthinkable happened. PSV won a free-kick on the left and Alex made amends for his earlier own goal by heading the cross past Lehmann. There were seven minutes to go and the Gunners now needed to score twice to stay in the competition. Fábregas tried his best but deep down he knew that there was no way back. Arsenal would not be repeating their 2006 Champions League final appearance; the Gunners' season was lying in tatters but they still needed a strong finish to ensure a Champions League place next season.

They beat Aston Villa 1–0 at Villa Park but found themselves on the wrong end of a 1–0 scoreline in midweek as Andy Johnson's late winner earned Everton the three points at Goodison Park. Arsenal stayed third as Liverpool could only manage a draw in an earlier kick-off, but that did little to improve the mood on the journey home.

International commitments gave Fábregas a welcome bolthole from the chaos at Arsenal. It allowed him to unwind a little with the rest of the Spanish camp and forget about the Gunners' plight. Spain faced Denmark and Iceland in crucial Euro 2008 qualifiers and, after the morale-denting losses to Northern Ireland and Sweden, Fábregas needed no reminding how important these fixtures were.

However, Cesc remained an unused substitute as Spain beat Denmark 2–1. Iniesta had taken his midfield role for this match, and the youngster was concerned he had dropped down the pecking order. Spain went on to make it two wins in four days but needed a late winner from Iniesta to clinch the victory. It was far from the team's best display, making it all the more surprising that Fábregas was left on the bench for the full 90 minutes for the second successive match.

Back in England, Arsenal were struggling to maintain momentum. A 4–1 defeat at Liverpool was followed by a home defeat to relegation-threatened West Ham. Fábregas' luck was well and truly out. He had struck the woodwork or been denied by brilliant saves so often during the campaign and against the Hammers he beat Robert Green with a fine drive, only to see the ball crash back off the crossbar. He also forced Green into a good save from a header. What more could he do? The team was struggling to score goals and a 0–0 draw in midweek with Newcastle only served to emphasise the crisis.

17

After one victory from their last six games prior to their clash with their bogey side Bolton, Arsenal desperately needed the three points to raise morale. Fortunately Fábregas chose this match to re-discover his scoring boots. Initially, it was a typical Arsenal home game. The visitors took the lead and the Gunners were desperately fighting back. Rosicky equalised and then, just after half-time, Fábregas stepped into the limelight to score his first Premiership goal of the season. He burst on to a through ball and calmly put the Gunners ahead. They hung on to the advantage and the Emirates was a much cheerier place.

No sooner had Cesc netted his first league goal of the season than he was on the scoresheet again. In the next home game, against Manchester City, he scored Arsenal's crucial second goal to set up a 3–1 victory. The ball fell to him 25 yards out and, with his confidence sky high, he fired into the net. At last he was producing complete midfield displays.

A trip to White Hart Lane should have brought a third consecutive win for the Gunners, but a late goal from Jermaine Jenas earned the home side a 2–2 draw. Fábregas' deliveries from set pieces had been immaculate all afternoon and he was the provider for both Arsenal goals.

Determined to finish the season strongly, the team pressed on. The 3–1 score at home to Fulham did not tell the full story as the Gunners needed two late goals to clinch the three points. They had one final opportunity to bask in the spotlight as Chelsea arrived on the penultimate weekend of the season, needing a victory to keep their title hopes alive. Anything less would send the Premiership trophy back to Manchester.

When Khalid Boulahrouz was sent off after fouling Baptista in the box just before half-time and Gilberto converted the spot-kick, it looked all over for Chelsea. The champions had a mountain to climb. Chelsea responded heroically in the second half and, led by Michael Essien, they threatened to defy the odds. The Ghanaian powered forward to head an equaliser, giving the Blues 20 minutes to keep their title dreams alive. But Fábregas was typically busy at the heart of the Arsenal midfield and twice created chances that could have won the match. In the end, they had to settle for a 1–1 draw.

The final match of the season was a 0–0 draw at Fratton Park against Portsmouth. After the emotions of the clash with Chelsea, the Gunners were not on top form, but there was still plenty of drama. Wenger fielded a young line-up, taking the chance to test some of his fledglings. Fábregas took his place in midfield and was influential in crafting the string of chances that Arsenal squandered in the first half. Baptista missed a penalty as well as a good chance from a Fábregas free-kick.

The draw with Portsmouth meant that the Gunners finished fourth in the Premiership table, a humiliating 21 points behind Manchester United. Arsenal had started the season poorly and had never threatened to join the title race, leaving United and Chelsea to fight for the trophy. Liverpool ended on the same points total as Arsenal, but took third place on goal difference. Once again they would have to get through a qualifying tie to secure their place in next season's Champions League.

On a positive note, it had been a good year for Cesc. He had been the brightest light in the Arsenal side on numerous occasions, and his passing and understanding with his team-mates was getting better and better. He had been superb in securing two victories over United during the campaign, and two draws against Chelsea. It showed just how much he loved the big occasion and how he refused to be intimidated by the prospect of facing other top-class players.

His displays were recognised when he came second to Cristiano Ronaldo as PFA Young Player of the Year but now he wanted a rest. He said, 'I am looking forward to this summer. Sometimes I do think I need one summer just to rest. I remember when I was 16 turning 17, I had seven weeks rest and I came back in pre-season refreshed and ready to go. That is what made the difference because I was a reserve player and I came into the first team in this period, and because I had rested I had a lot of energy and power.' The trouble was, now he had international duty.

Shortly after the end of the Premiership season, Fábregas was once more in action with Spain. He did not feature in the 2–0 win away to Latvia but returned to the starting line-up in Liechtenstein. He was replaced after 68 minutes, but not before he had conjured Spain's opening goal for Villa. The 2–0 victory over Liechtenstein made it four qualifying wins in a row and the team's prospects looked very bright.

Any hopes Fábregas may have had of spending a few peaceful weeks following international duty were dashed when reports began to circulate linking him with a move to Real Madrid. Cesc had wanted to switch off from football and these rumours were far from welcome. When he eventually spoke on the matter, he made it clear that he had no plans to leave Arsenal. He said, 'I am only 20 and all I have to do is enjoy my football and improve, and I want to do that with this team. I will try to win titles with Arsenal and give my all to Arsène Wenger. I will always be grateful to him for giving me my chance.'

Cesc might have stayed at the Emirates but, during the summer of 2007, the inevitable happened: Thierry Henry completed his on-off move to Barcelona for £16.2 million. The striker's departure opened the way for Fábregas to take control of the team's passing style. As Andy Dunn of the *People* put it: 'Henry is the history of Wenger's reign, Fábregas is the future.'

18

The media were not predicting big things from Arsenal's young squad for the next season, but Wenger thought they could 'win the Premiership and win all kinds of trophies they want to win. The hunger in the team is strong, my hunger is stronger than ever and the talent and the potential of the team are very high.'

In an interview with *Four Four Two*, Wenger also revealed: 'When you have a player of his [Henry's] importance with such a young team, the play was always going to go through him. When he wanted the ball, he got the ball. Now he's not there any more, everybody has to take the initiative and express themselves a little bit more.'

Fábregas agreed with Wenger, telling the *Guardian*: 'Thierry is the best I've ever played with. There's no doubt. But there was this other factor. When I came I felt I was low and he was high and for a long time I was intimidated. When I had the ball I felt I had no choice but to look for him. He has such a strong character that he almost made you feel this way. I needed him to say, "Look, you don't always have to play the ball to me." Once he said that, I was free and I gave him even more assists.'

The major component missing from Fábregas' midfield displays in the past few years had been a lack of goals and now he had been given a greater licence to shoot. He vowed to improve this area of his game and better the measly four goals he had scored during the last campaign. Two of those goals had come in a Champions League qualifier in August and the other two were in April; the long drought in between needed to be addressed.

Fábregas revealed in an interview with Jonathan Northcroft of *The Sunday Times*, that Wenger gave him some guidance prior to the start of the campaign: 'The boss told me, "You have to be calm." He showed me a video tape and said, "See? You have more time than you think." Before there was something in my head saying "Score!" and I wanted to do things too quick, without thinking.'

Wenger did not make big-name signings to replace Henry, preferring to spread the money around on Croatian international Eduardo Da Silva and French full-back Bacary Sagna. Meanwhile their fellow title challengers were looking strong. Manchester United had been the biggest spenders, adding youngsters Nani and Anderson and England international Owen Hargreaves. Ferguson also completed a loan move for Argentine Carlos Tevez, who had been at the centre of controversy during his stint at West Ham.

At Anfield, Liverpool were welcoming several new faces, including the Spanish striker Fernando Torres. Cesc knew all about Torres' quality from his involvement in the international squad and felt the former Atletico Madrid forward would be a huge success on Merseyside. Chelsea, meanwhile, had their quietest summer since the arrival of Abramovich, with Florent Malouda, costing around £13.5 million, the only big-money addition to the squad.

The mood around the Emirates was not helped by some negative comments from within the Arsenal dressing room. Among the dissenters was Gallas, who questioned the club's ambition in the wake of Henry's departure: 'What is sure is that several players are questioning the club's future. Around us, all the teams are recruiting, but what is planned to compensate for the departure of Henry? It is necessary to recruit players of reputation because young players have many qualities but the season is very long.' Gallas' outburst was strangely rewarded in due course with the captain's armband.

The season began at home to Fulham but the team made a far from convincing start with the visitors grabbing a very early lead. Fábregas and his team-mates had to dig deep to fight back and they completed a dramatic turnaround with just minutes remaining.

Arsenal made a strong start to their Champions League campaign, winning 2–0 in the first leg of their qualifier against Sparta Prague, a game that saw Cesc open his goal-scoring account for the season, netting Arsenal's first goal and making life easier for the return leg at the Emirates.

Back in the Premiership, a 1–1 draw at Blackburn was a frustrating result because the Gunners had dominated large chunks of the match. But there was no time to dwell on the lost points. Fábregas was off to Athens where he was a late sub as Spain lost 3–2 to Grece. He was disappointed at not starting and wondered whether playing his club football outside Spain really was hindering his chances at international level.

The appointment of former England coach Sven Goran Eriksson as manager of Manchester City added spice to their visit to the Emirates. Arsenal fans groaned in disbelief when van Persie's penalty was saved by Kasper Schmeichel with 25 minutes to go. Fortunately, Fábregas refused to accept a 0–0 score and on one of his increasingly regular bursts from midfield, the Spaniard decided the match in the 80th minute with a crisp finish.

After the match, Wenger said, 'Cesc will score more goals. But this was a goal that did not come from a chance. And while other midfielders may score more, Cesc contributes more in the way of assists.' The Spaniard was the clear choice as Man of the Match for his role in the narrow win, and hoped it would be the first of many as he headed for the dressing room with a bottle of champagne in his hands.

In an interview with the *Guardian*, Fábregas talked about his whirlwind career to date: 'Next week it will be four years since I left Barcelona for Arsenal. Everything has come so quickly that it's unbelievable. I am proud of how I coped, but I knew what I wanted even before I came here. I knew if I had to be alone for two years then I could do it – as long as it meant first-team football. If I could show everybody what I could do on the pitch then there would be no problem at all with the loneliness.'

Another confident defensive display kept Sparta Prague at bay, the 3–0 score putting Arsenal into the group stage. Rested by Wenger, Fábregas came off the bench to score Arsenal's second late on. The following weekend he took his goal tally to four, netting Arsenal's second in a 3–1 victory. The manager celebrated by signing a new, four-year contract.

The only frustration for Cesc at this stage of the season was the lack of opportunities he received from Aragones on the international stage. Named in the Spanish squad to face Iceland, Fábregas could only watch from the bench as Spain collected a 1–1 draw from the trip. He had not played for even one minute in four of the last five qualifiers and was a little baffled by his lack of opportunities. A few days later, yet another 90 minutes on the sidelines added to the disappointment – this time Spain picked up a win in his absence, beating Latvia 2–0 in Oviedo.

Back in England, the Gunners travelled the short distance to their north London rivals Spurs who were struggling, with manager Martin Jol under fire. It would be one of the toughest tests of this new-look Arsenal side. Fábregas went toe-to-toe with fellow fledglings Jermaine Jenas and Tom Huddlestone and, once again, proved his worth. With the Gunners trailing to a Gareth Bale strike, Fábregas refused to be flustered and would not be moved from his usual patient, passing approach. Gradually, Arsenal wore Tottenham down and Adebayor equalised.

Then came a moment that illustrated just how far Fábregas had developed. Collecting the ball just inside the Tottenham half, he was not closed down. As no challenge arrived, he surged towards goal and unleashed a ferocious strike that left Paul Robinson with no chance. Fábregas raced over to the Arsenal fans to celebrate pursued by his team-mates. Adebayor struck an impressive third goal late on as the team kept their unbeaten run alive.

In an article in the *Daily Mirror*, Martin Lipton relayed Wenger's praise for Fábregas: 'If it becomes hectic, he keeps his head and cools the game down. Suddenly he finds a good pass and gets you out of tight situations.' Lipton himself called Fábregas 'the boy-man' and added that he 'may only be 20, but in his head he is already 32, chillingly calm amid the maelstrom and utterly outstanding.'

Arsenal were winning over the doubters, and pundits who had written off their title hopes were being forced to re-think their opinion. For his part, Fábregas had seen nothing in the first few months of the season to persuade him that Arsenal were not good enough to win a trophy: 'I believe we can win one of the major ones, like the Premier League or the Champions League. It has been two years since we have won a trophy and that is too long for Arsenal. I cannot even think about a third year like that. We have to be lucky with injuries and things like that. But we have learned together, we have gained experience together. We are all winners. Even if it means we stay at home every night and just concentrate on football, then that is what we have to do.'

19

The Champions League group stages started with a home match against Sevilla, a side famed for their attacking play. Unfortunately for the Spaniards, they met an Arsenal side on top form. Fábregas was once again in the thick of the action. His strike was deflected into the net by defender Julien Escude to give the Gunners the lead just before the half-hour mark. Then his free-kick created a chance for van Persie who made it 2–0. To put the icing on the cake, Fábregas was also involved in the build-up for the third goal, scored by new boy Eduardo.

It was great timing on the Spaniard's part. Prior to the match, Wenger had compared Fábregas to one of France's greatest ever players, Michel Platini. 'His vision is comparable to Platini. Cesc has it all in front of him, but he has a vision. He will still develop. I remember Platini was more of a striker and Cesc is more of a midfielder. He is adding that element to his game, but Platini had more of a striker's mentality. Cesc is a guy who likes to be at the heart of things.'

The following weekend, Fábregas struck again. Premiership newcomers Derby received little sympathy at the Emirates as the Gunners smashed five goals past them, with Adebayor bagging a hat-trick. Cesc scored Arsenal's fourth and played some sumptuous passes, one of which released Adebayor for the first goal of the afternoon.

Having sat out Arsenal's Carling Cup victory over Sam Allardyce's Newcastle, Fábregas returned to the fray against

West Ham at Upton Park, keen to protect the Gunners' unbeaten start to the campaign. The previous season the team had suffered a 1–0 defeat away to the Hammers in the match that saw Arsène Wenger and Alan Pardew apparently squaring up to one another on the touchline. This time Arsenal recorded a 1–0 win.

A fifth consecutive clean sheet followed away to Steaua Bucharest in Europe in a match where Fábregas should have added to his goals tally, but he wasted one glorious opportunity. Instead, Van Persie struck with 14 minutes to go to earn Arsenal a 1–0 victory and then continued his hot streak with two goals the following weekend in a 3–2 win against Roy Keane's Sunderland. The three points put Arsenal top of the table again.

October saw Arsenal fighting off speculation linking Cesc with a move to Barcelona. His agent, Joseba Diaz, did little to ease the concern among Gunners fans: 'I have spoken with Cesc and we are not aware of any interest from Barça. And if they do have interest, hopefully they do because they are a great club, who play great football and Cesc was very happy there.' Diaz also spread the news in Madrid-based Spanish magazine *Marca*, saying, 'What will come, will come. If we received an offer from Barcelona, clearly we would listen to it. It is the club which taught Cesc everything and it would be a compliment if that happened.'

Fábregas simply focused on his football and linked up with his Spanish colleagues during the international break. Aragones finally restored him to the starting line-up against Denmark in the latest Euro 2008 qualifier, and the team's performance seemed to go up a notch as they won 3–1 away from home. The three points pushed Spain closer to sealing a place at Euro 2008, but Sweden and surprise package Northern Ireland – who had both beaten Fábregas and company last year – were also chasing a spot at the tournament.

Then, on 20 October, after a two-week break, the Gunners welcomed Bolton to the Emirates. Before kick-off Fábregas and Wenger received warm applause from the Arsenal supporters as they collected their player and manager of the month awards. Bolton proved stubborn opponents but eventually, in the final half hour, Arsenal wore them down. First, Kolo Toure fired home a free-kick after a foul on Fábregas and then Rosicky made sure of the points late on.

The Gunners' superb start to the season inevitably led to comparisons with the 'Invincibles'. This merely added pressure so Cesc tried to shrug off the topic when speaking to the media: 'We don't want to listen to talk that we are "Invincibles" because we have had a good run of results. We have to go for the big competitions and I would say that the Premier League is the hardest.'

The impressive sequence of results showed no signs of ending. Slavia Prague were torn to shreds in a 7–0 win with Fábregas back among the goals, scoring twice. But, back in domestic action, Liverpool provided the Gunners with their first big test of the season. Both sides were unbeaten in the Premiership and it promised to be a tense afternoon at Anfield. Arsenal's hopes took a knock when Steven Gerrard struck a firm free-kick past Almunia to give the home side the lead but, from then on, the Londoners dominated. Fábregas took control of midfield and Liverpool were forced to play like the away side as they retreated into their own half.

Fábregas, with Hleb, gradually began to find space in the final third, but time was against Arsenal. Liverpool were still leading as the game entered the final 15 minutes. Sensing the Gunners' unbeaten run was in serious jeopardy, Fábregas emerged to make his latest vital contribution. Picked out cleverly by Hleb's pass, Cesc burst beyond the Liverpool back four and slotted the ball under the advancing Reina with 10 minutes to go. There was still time for Fábregas to pop up again in the Liverpool area, but this time his shot cruelly smashed against the post and rebounded to safety. The final whistle blew and the Gunners grudgingly accepted the 1–1 score.

Cesc had seen his fair share of Manchester United already in his short career, but the clash between Arsenal and United at the Emirates the following weekend promised to be another classic. And this time, he would take on an even more prominent role in the action. United were putting a shaky start to the season behind them. Draws with Reading and Portsmouth, followed by a 1–0 derby loss to Manchester City, had put Sir Alex Ferguson's side under intense scrutiny. Now, though, with Rooney, Ronaldo and Tevez striking up better understandings, the champions were back level on points with Arsenal at the top of the table.

The expectations on Cesc's shoulders were cranked up a notch by glowing comments made by Emmanuel Adebayor in the build-up to the game. The Togo striker told the press: 'At the moment, Cesc is the best in the world. It's between him and Barcelona's Lionel Messi. He's a great player, too, but, for me, it's Cesc Fábregas. It's not just because he's my team-mate, but the way he plays. Absolutely fantastic.'

Fábregas himself made a couple of comments pre-match, which showed the respect he and his team-mates had for the Old Trafford outfit. In what could be seen as a sideswipe at Chelsea and Liverpool, Cesc said, 'I love the way United play. They are a great side. I always watch them and they are the only team I really like watching in England every week.'

Midfield was where this match would be won or lost with Fábregas and Flamini locking horns with Hargreaves and Anderson. All four midfielders were tireless runners and the battle was guaranteed to mean a gruelling 90 minutes for all involved. In an even first half, Fábregas struggled to find his usual rhythm as United swarmed around him in midfield. As a result, Arsenal could not break the visitors down and the creativity that had cut through the likes of Derby and Tottenham was sadly missing. Worse was to follow as the champions took the lead just before half-time. Gallas diverted Rooney's effort into the net.

Wenger roused the team during the interval and Fábregas responded in an all-action second half. After only three minutes he put Arsenal level. A neat build-up gave Adebayor a good chance. Van der Sar smothered his effort, but the loose ball eventually found its way to Fábregas who calmly passed the ball into the net. The goal illustrated perfectly the youngster's improvements and Fábregas admitted in *The Sunday Times*: 'Last year my body would have gone towards the floor and the ball would have gone into the stand.'

The momentum was now with the Gunners and Fábregas continued to burst forward. As the game entered the final 10 minutes, both sides looked weary but the drama was only just beginning. A great run by Patrice Evra presented Ronaldo with a simple opportunity. He beat Almunia and United were eight minutes away from a massive victory but the Gunners would not throw in the towel. Fábregas drove his colleagues forward in search of a late equaliser and a cross from the left sparked chaos in the United box. Eventually, the ball broke to Gallas who lashed a smart strike goalwards. Van der Sar clawed the shot out, but the officials correctly ruled it had crossed the line. Arsenal had salvaged a point and remained top of the Premiership with a vital game in hand.

With the Gunners comfortably placed in Group H, Wenger rested Fábregas for the Champions League game against Slavia Prague and gave some of the squad's fringe players a run out. A point from the 0–0 draw was enough to put Arsenal through to the second round of the competition.

While his team-mates made heavy weather of their fixture in Prague, Fábregas took the chance to head back to Barcelona along with Hleb, who had also been rested. Cesc has struck up many friendships during his time at Arsenal, but his bond with Hleb was particularly strong. They were on the same wavelength on and off the pitch and, with their manager's blessing, the duo travelled to Spain to watch Barcelona face Rangers in their Champions League. Fábregas was able to meet up with friends and family as well as make use of his Barça season ticket. Then it was back to work.

20

The break meant that Fábregas was fresh for a Monday night trip to Reading. United had won at the weekend to go top of the table but Arsenal overpowered the Royals 3–1 to reclaim top spot. The only low point that night for the Spaniard was the yellow card he picked up in the second half – his fifth of the season – earning him a one-match ban.

The international break then saw Cesc link up with his colleagues for the final two Euro 2008 qualifiers. He helped Spain pick up a 3–0 victory over the Swedes in Madrid that guaranteed their place at the summer's showpiece. It was a special moment. Cesc played in a more advanced role on the night – more reminiscent of the position he played for Spain's youth teams – and was involved in the opening goal, flicking on Xavi's corner for defender Joan Capdevila to score. There was nothing at stake for Spain in their last group game, but they found the desire to beat Northern Ireland 1–0 in Las Palmas, ending Irish hopes of a place in the finals. Meanwhile, England also failed to qualify.

Two weeks after the international fixtures, Arsenal picked up another three points against Wigan and then heard the good news that United had lost 1–0 at Bolton. If Arsenal could win their game in hand, they'd go six points clear at the top. They had some Champions League business to attend to first as Sevilla still hoped to take away top spot in the group after Arsenal's 0–0 draw in Prague. Despite taking the lead, Fábregas and company were outplayed by Sevilla, who scored twice in 10 minutes to lead 2–1 at the break. In the second half, Fábregas was forced to limp off after suffering a hamstring injury. It had not been one of his better displays and it made the Gunners' task even harder. Kanoute eventually sealed the contest 3–1 with a late penalty. It was the Gunners' first loss of the season and there was plenty of frustration in the Arsenal camp. Sevilla were now in the driving seat and when the Spaniards beat Slavia Prague, Arsenal had to accept second place in the group and the prospect of a much tougher second-round tie.

Switching his attention to the international scene momentarily in late November, Fábregas watched with interest as the 2010 World Cup qualifying groups were drawn. Aragones' men were placed in Group 5 and had to face Turkey, Belgium, Bosnia and Herzegovina, Armenia and Estonia. If the Turks were on song they might prove a serious threat, but otherwise it seemed like plain-sailing.

Back in the league, December began well for Arsenal with a 2–1 win over Aston Villa, but the next couple of weeks highlighted the effect of Fábregas' enforced absence. His hamstring problem kept him out of the matches at Newcastle and Middlesbrough and, with van Persie also missing, the Gunners collected just one point out of a possible six. The Gunners were now only a point ahead of United.

Fábregas worked to regain full fitness ahead of what was billed as 'Grand Slam Sunday' with United facing Liverpool, then Arsenal taking on Chelsea. It promised to be a pivotal weekend in the title race. After hard work by the physios, Cesc was passed fit for the match against the Blues. As the players completed their final preparations before the game, news filtered through of United's 1–0 win at Anfield, courtesy of a Carlos Tevez goal. Whether they admitted it or not, this result put more pressure on the Gunners as they walked out in front of a noisy Emirates crowd.

Recent encounters between Arsenal and Chelsea had been fiery affairs and this proved to be no different. Tackles flew in, players swarmed around the referee and there was plenty of pushing and shoving. Fábregas was in the thick of the action and reacted furiously to a nasty challenge by Chelsea skipper John Terry. The whistle had already blown for a free-kick when Terry launched himself into the tackle. The Spaniard was looking unhappy about it. This led to more bitter arguing and Emmanuel Eboue was guilty of a bad challenge which resulted in Terry limping from the field.

This was the turning point. Tal Ben Haim replaced Terry and, from that moment on, Chelsea never looked as composed. The decisive moment arrived just before half-time. Fábregas sent a corner into the Blues' penalty area, Petr Cech misjudged the flight of the ball and Gallas headed the Gunners into the lead. Chelsea tried to fight back in the second half, creating several openings, one of which was badly missed by Shaun Wright-Phillips. Late on, Cesc and Ashley Cole looked like they might come to blows after the Spaniard fouled Cole from behind. Referee Alan Wiley calmed the situation and booked Fábregas. The cautions were totting up for him. He was getting dangerously close to 10 yellow cards which would mean a two-match ban. Arsenal didn't want to lose him in the title run-in.

Wenger's side should have extended their advantage, but held on for a 1–0 victory and three vital points. It was their first win over Chelsea since early 2004. Cesc had managed to play the full 90 minutes on his return from injury and the Gunners were still top with the busy Christmas programme approaching.

Meanwhile, Fábregas was glued to the television as the Euro 2008 groups were drawn. Spain were drawn in Group D with the holders Greece, Russia and Sweden. It was arguably the easiest of the four groups, and certainly a lot easier than Group C which contained World Cup holders Italy, with France, Holland and Romania. There was more suspense with the Champions League second-round draw. Arsenal were paired with the reigning champions AC Milan.

The Premiership campaign continued with a north London derby. Tottenham had replaced former boss Martin Jol with Spaniard Juande Ramos, the man in charge of Sevilla when they beat Arsenal. Under him, Spurs had begun to climb the table and it promised to be an interesting afternoon at the Emirates. After a tight, goalless first half, the Gunners seized the initiative with Fábregas at the heart of the action. His clever backheel found Adebayor, who placed his shot past Paul Robinson to give Arsenal the lead. Tottenham did not surrender though. Instead, they stunned the Emirates crowd by first equalising through Dimitar Berbatov after 66 minutes and then winning a penalty for a foul by Toure on the Bulgarian striker. To Arsenal's relief Alumnia saved Robbie Keane's spot-kick and, shortly afterwards, substitute Nicklas Bendtner headed the winner for the Gunners from Fábregas' pinpoint corner.

Against Portsmouth on Boxing Day, the Spaniard had a quiet game as Harry Redknapp's side frustrated Arsenal on the way to a deserved 0–0 draw. United's victory earlier in the day gave them a one-point lead at the top and took the edge off the Christmas festivities. The media waited with interest to see how Arsenal responded to losing their top spot. How much character was there in this young side?

Initially, the signs did not look good and eager reporters were reaching for their notepads as the Gunners soon fell behind to Everton. The second half was all Arsenal and they emphatically answered any questions about their spirit and character. Two goals from Eduardo put the Gunners ahead before the hour and Wenger looked far more relaxed in the technical area. Bendtner then received a second yellow card for a poor challenge on Andy Johnson leaving his team-mates to protect their lead with 10 men. Substitute Adebayor made it 3–1 and the pressure was eased.

There was still time for Cesc to influence the action again and, in the 84th minute, he was struck by the arm of fellow Spaniard Mikel Arteta, who was shown a red card. The Everton players were incensed by Fábregas' reaction, feeling he had exaggerated the contact, and this led to pushing and shoving as frustrations boiled over. When Cesc was booked shortly after, Wenger substituted the Spaniard to ensure he did not lose his temper in the dying moments. Arsène brought on Rosicky who made it 4–1 before the close. David Moyes questioned Fábregas' reaction to the supposed elbow from Arteta. 'I hope his jaw is OK. He went down as if it was broken,' the Everton boss said sarcastically. Cesc wasn't too impressed.

Manchester United had lost 2–1 at West Ham that afternoon, sparking a double celebration in the Arsenal dressing room. They were top of the table once again but now it was their turn to take on the Hammers. They had none of United's problems, scoring twice in the first 20 minutes to clinch a 2–0 win. Fábregas set up the opening goal for Eduardo with a clever lofted pass and the Croatian did the rest. Adebayor then scored an excellent second to leave the Hammers with too much to do. United also won and so the Gunners' lead at the top remained two points.

Arsenal began their FA Cup campaign away to Burnley. Wenger opted to rest Cesc after the hectic Christmas fixture list. Eduardo continued his hot streak with a goal in the ninth minute and Bendtner sealed the points with 15 minutes to go. Fábregas' break continued as the Gunners drew 1–1 in the first leg of the Carling Cup semi-final against Spurs but he returned for the league clash with Birmingham. It was a frustrating afternoon with the Midlands side managing to equalise Adebayor's opener and they hung on for a point. To make matters worse, United later won 6–0 at home to Newcastle and leapfrogged Arsenal into top spot. It was a fight to the finish. The following weekend Arsenal trashed Fulham 3–0 and United countered with a 2–0 win at Reading.

Wenger included Fábregas and some of his other first-team players in the squad for the second leg of their semi-final against Spurs. Cesc came off the bench after 18 minutes following an injury to Denilson with Spurs already a goal up, but there was little the Spaniard could do against a buoyant home side who ran out 5–1 winners. Arsenal had been well and truly rattled and Fábregas again found himself trudging off at the final whistle with his head hung in dismay.

There was little time to dwell on this setback. Arsenal had an FA Cup tie against a Newcastle side lifted by the return of Kevin Keegan as their manager. The Gunners managed to spoil 'King Kevin's' return to the Magpie's hot seat, easing into the fifth round with a 3–0 win. The draw then paired Arsenal with Manchester United, a match worthy of the final but, before that, Fábregas lined up against Newcastle again in midweek in the league. There was plenty of speculation about where the title would end up but Cesc told the media: 'We do not have to look at the others, we have to look at ourselves – if we win every game, we will be champions.' Arsenal kept up the pressure, securing their second 3–0 win over Newcastle in the space of four days with Cesc back among the goals.

That success was followed by a 3–1 win at Manchester City and, with United only picking up a point at Tottenham, Arsenal were top again. Fábregas told the press: 'Even though we are still young, we have shown the world what we can do. We have had to learn to be patient, and now we have taken our chance. We would be very disappointed if we didn't win it [the title]. That's certain.' But he wasn't taking

anything for granted and pointed out that Chelsea, now under Avram Grant, were only six points behind the Gunners: 'There's not only Manchester United, there's also Chelsea. We'll see what happens, but I'm sure they'll be there at the end.'

21

Fábregas linked up with his international colleagues for a friendly against France in Malaga. Though publicly the talk of revenge for the World Cup defeat was dismissed, Cesc and his team-mates wanted to put one over on the French. The youngster began the match on the bench, but came on with the score goalless and helped his colleagues to a 1–0 victory.

Back in England, Cesc focused on Arsenal again and their bid for silverware. Next for the Gunners was a home game against Blackburn. Because it was a Monday night fixture Cesc and his team-mates had already seen United lose a Manchester derby on the Sunday afternoon. With Chelsea drawing 0-0 with Liverpool it was a chance for Arsenal to cash in.

Prior to the Rovers game, and no doubt mindful of the spat with Mark Hughes the last time the sides met, Wenger told the media how impressed he was with the growing maturity of Fábregas: 'Cesc has behaved remarkably well this season, I cannot remember one incident. There was maybe a stage six months ago, where he went a bit the wrong way but he corrected that very well, without any special management from me. He apologised and from then on there have been no problems with him. He is so intelligent he realised that is not the way he wanted to go.'

Predictably, Arsenal came out strongly, eager to send a message to United. Senderos scored from a corner within four minutes and it looked like Fábregas – who was playing on the right of midfield – and his colleagues would go on to secure an easy win. However Blackburn created several decent chances and started to make life tough for the Gunners, but Adebayor finally sealed the win in stoppage time. The only low point on the night was a booking for Fábregas that took his tally for the season to nine: one more caution would bring a two-match suspension. The Arsenal players formed their customary post-match huddle and celebrated their five-point lead at the top of the table.

Fábregas hit the headlines when news of a contract extension offer from Arsenal reached the media. Andrew Dillon of the *Sun* wrote: 'Cesc Fábregas will rocket to the top of Arsenal's pay league with an amazing new deal worth £33 million. Gunners manager Arsène Wenger wants the Spanish midfielder, 20, to commit until 2016 by signing a two-year extension to his current contract.' The newspaper also speculated as to Fábregas' pay increase, suggesting that the player's wage might jump from £50,000 a week to £80,000. It showed how valuable the Spaniard had become to the club.

The following weekend saw the Gunners in FA Cup action again as the big games kept coming. And it did not get much bigger than Manchester United away. With both sides eyeing up a possible treble, this tie would end the dream for one of them. The United-Arsenal clash was by far the most intriguing of the round. An easier tie would have allowed Wenger and Ferguson to rest players ahead of European commitments, but neither was willing to field heavily weakened sides for such a significant match.

Nobody could have predicted what happened next. Fábregas and his team-mates never got going and Ferguson's side gave them a 4–0 hammering and it could, and should, have been more. The Spaniard put in one of his worst performances of the season as United looked the hungrier side. Loose balls in midfield were seized upon by the men in red and, for the second time that season, the Brazilian Anderson did an effective job by overshadowing Fábregas in their midfield duel.

Cesc was well aware that he and his team-mates had to be careful that their season did not slide downhill. He recalled how Arsenal had lost out in the Carling Cup final the previous season, and had followed that with FA Cup and Champions League exits in quick succession. He knew the whole complexion of a season could change dramatically in a matter of weeks. The Gunners were out of both domestic cup competitions and the players were under more pressure to win the Premiership and the Champions League.

Arsenal clearly needed to shrug off the disappointment of their performance at Old Trafford before facing AC Milan in the Champions League. It promised to be a fascinating duel as Arsenal squared off against the reigning European champions. While most of the talk surrounding Milan revolved around Brazilian star Kaka and his youthful compatriot Alexandre Pato, those who watched them regularly knew that the midfield areas would be crucial. Most importantly, Fábregas needed to get close to Andrea Pirlo, the deep-lying Italian playmaker. Pirlo's effortless passing and calm temperament had been the driving force behind many of the club's triumphs, and anyone who watched the 2006 World Cup would have noticed the effect he had on his team-mates. If Fábregas could win the battle with Pirlo, Arsenal would surely stand an excellent chance of progressing to the quarter-finals.

It was a battle of youth against experience. Milan still contained players like Paolo Maldini, who had made his Serie A debut two years before Cesc was born and his 1,000th Milan appearance the weekend before the first leg. However, the Brazilian striker Ronaldo had been ruled out for the Italian giants with a knee injury and Milan did not look as deadly up front without him, especially as Kaka and Pato went into the game carrying injuries.

As usual, Fábregas was sought out by the media pre-match for his verdict on the game and Arsenal's chances of victory. Cesc explained: 'Milan are maybe not doing too well in Serie A, but they are different in the Champions League. They have one of the strongest midfields in the world. We all know that Italian teams know how to play these kinds of games, but we're not scared of anything. We respect them a lot because they are a great side with great players who have won nearly everything. We want to be like them one day and this is one of the days where you can show you are ready for a big future.' He added that the loss to United would not be weighing on his mind: 'Yes, the 4–0 was difficult to understand. I felt very bad. But the players will bounce back.'

It turned out to be a night of frustration for the home side as Milan produced a resolute defensive display so typical of Italian sides. The match ended 0–0, but Fábregas knew that Arsenal should have scored at least a couple of goals. Eboue missed a decent opening, Fábregas twice forced saves from goalkeeper Zeljko Kalac and then Adebayor squandered the best chance of the night, heading against the bar from just yards out.

Cesc told the media post-match that the Arsenal players were disappointed not to have won, but still remained confident of finishing the job in Italy: 'After a big defeat against Manchester United at the weekend we came back strong. We had quite a lot of chances, but in football you have to take them. Hopefully, we won't regret it and we can go there, play the same way and I am sure we can win. If we can score a goal I think we have a good opportunity to go through.'

It set things up beautifully for the second leg in the San Siro. Milan were favourites but if Arsenal could score an away goal...

Arsenal went back to the Premiership, at Birmingham. This was the business end of the season. Fábregas and his team-mates were determined to come flying out of the traps and extend their lead at the top to eight points before United took on Newcastle later that day. Just minutes into game Eduardo suffered a bad challenge by defender Martin Taylor that left his leg horrifically shattered. As Fábregas and his team-mates looked on in dismay, the striker was stretchered from the field after lengthy treatment. Taylor was sent off for the tackle, but it was the Gunners who suffered more from the incident.

Arsenal were noticeably shaken to see their friend in such pain and they struggled to find their usual form. James McFadden gave the home side the lead, but a Walcott brace looked to have clinched the points for Arsenal. However, there was another twist as Birmingham managed to snatch a 2–2 draw after Clichy conceded a late penalty. It sparked several minutes of mayhem as Gallas ranted at Clichy and then stormed up to the other end of the pitch and sat down. McFadden scored from the spot and then Wenger had to coax the distraught Gallas off the pitch at the final whistle. It was undoubtedly Arsenal's least memorable weekend of the season. United's 5–1 demolition of Newcastle completed a miserable day for the Gunners as their lead was cut to three points. Even worse, the following weekend the gap was reduced to a single point as Arsenal could only draw at home to Aston Villa while United won with ease at Fulham. In truth, it could have been worse for Fábregas as the Gunners needed a late equaliser to salvage their draw. Things were getting shaky.

22

As the Gunners prepared to fly over to Italy for the massive second leg, nobody needed to remind them that they would have to find a better performance against Milan. No English team had won in the San Siro and Manchester United had been decimated there in the previous season's semi-final. The match was, in many ways, a carbon copy of the first leg. After a nervy start, Arsenal dominated possession with Fábregas and Hleb heavily involved in some beautiful passing moves. Meanwhile, the Italians were content to soak up the pressure and wait for their chance to strike. But it never came as the Gunners produced their most impressive display of the campaign.

Such was Arsenal's superiority it was easy to forget that Milan were the reigning champions. Adebayor was always dangerous while Senderos and Eboue also had good chances in front of goal. To add to the frustration, referee Konrad Plautz denied the visitors a clear free-kick on the edge of the area and incredibly booked Hleb for diving instead. For the champions, Kaka gave brief glimpses of his talent but he was well shackled by Fábregas and Flamini, while Inzaghi and Pato rarely worried Gallas and Toure.

With time running out, it looked as though Milan had once again survived the Arsenal onslaught and both managers must have begun to consider extra-time. Yet Fábregas had no such thoughts. With six minutes to go, he picked the ball up inside the Milan half and drove towards goal as defenders backed away. With limited support, he opted to shoot from distance and sent a skidding 30-yard shot beyond Kalac's dive into the bottom corner. You could hear a pin drop in the San Siro as Fábregas, arms outstretched, raced off to celebrate. There was no way back for Milan. Arsenal were going through to the quarter-finals. Adebayor added a second for good measure, but it was Cesc who stole the headlines. He was overwhelmed as he spoke to the media after the match: 'This is a dream come true. But this is just the beginning. We are now in the quarter-finals, but we have not done anything. It is just one more step.'

Back in the Premiership Arsenal continued to falter. A 0–0 draw away to Wigan was followed by a 1–1 deadlock at home to Middlesbrough. Meanwhile, United took full advantage and their victory over Bolton put them three points ahead of the Gunners. The following weekend was the second coming of Grand Slam Sunday, but it came at the wrong time for the out-of-sorts Arsenal players. They had got the better of Chelsea earlier in the season while United had overcome Liverpool. Now they would have to do it all again. At Old Trafford, Ferguson's side trounced Liverpool 3–0, heaping pressure on both Arsenal and Chelsea.

After a tight first half at Stamford Bridge, Fábregas and his team-mates took the lead just before the hour mark. Cesc's inch-perfect corner was headed home by Sagna. It looked as though Arsenal might end their rotten Premiership run with a massive three points. But Chelsea still had their own title intentions and, in Drogba, they had a striker capable of turning the game on its head. He scored twice in nine minutes to leave the Gunners totally floored. Arsenal were six points behind United and now one behind Chelsea.

Confidence within the side had been visibly shaken by the poor run of results and a trip to Bolton the following Saturday was the last thing Arsenal needed. Initial worries were confirmed as the Gunners found themselves trailing 2–0 at half-time and down to 10 men after Diaby's dismissal. However, at last the character of the Arsenal side shone through. To his credit, Fábregas bounced back from a poor first half to help lead the charge. Goals from Gallas and van Persie – from the penalty spot – made it 2–2 before Cesc burst onto Hleb's cut-back and saw his shot deflected into the net for a late winner. Arsenal were still in the title race. The mood was dampened slightly by United's 4–0 victory over Aston Villa later in the day, but Fábregas was still delighted with the team's spirited comeback.

April was always going to be a tricky month, starting with three games against rivals Liverpool, two legs of the Champions League quarter-final separated by a home Premiership fixture. The Champions League home tie came first and was a thoroughly frustrating experience. Despite Fábregas playing a part in Adebayor's 23rd-minute opener, Arsenal were unable to hold on to the lead and had to settle for a 1–1 draw, though Fábregas went close with a late header. Three days later the sides met again in the Premiership. Once more they couldn't be separated, drawing 1–1. This time, a Crouch strike was cancelled out by a Bendtner header from yet another Fábregas free-kick. The goals may have dried up for the Spaniard, but the vital assists certainly had not.

Fábregas was in action again three days later for his third game in less than a week. Exhaustion was certainly catching up with the Spaniard and he was unable to prevent Arsenal from crashing out of the Champions League with a 4–2 defeat to Liverpool at Anfield. Arsenal's general tiredness was clear for all to see as they were undone by late goals from Gerrard and Babel. One trophy gone, but one still just about possible for Fábregas and Arsenal.

But even this possibility did not last long. Arsenal were

beaten 2–1 at home by future champions Manchester United five days later. Fábregas played his fourth full game in 11 days and, despite some majestic moments in the Gunners' strong start, he faded badly in the second half as defensive vulnerability rocked the Londoners again. Adebayor put Arsenal ahead after 48 minutes but a Ronaldo penalty and a fine Hargreaves free-kick won the game for Manchester United. Fábregas' season was all but over.

Arsenal won their last four league games but it was all in vain as they finished in third place, two points behind Chelsea and four behind Manchester United. Fábregas only played two of these last four games with Wenger giving his midfield playmaker a well-earned rest. The Spaniard played full games against Reading and Derby but sat out Arsenal's final, ultimately meaningless games against Everton and Sunderland.

It was a sad end to an extremely promising season for Arsenal, but Fábregas was at least rewarded at the end of season awards. Nominated for both PFA Player of the Year and PFA Young Player of the Year, he went on to win the latter and a place in the PFA Team of the Year. Typically modest and generous, the Spaniard dedicated the award to his team-mates: 'I am very proud because it is always satisfying for yourself, but all the team worked really hard this season and it's been disappointing at the end.'

The Spaniard finished the Premiership season with nine goals in 32 games and, most importantly, 19 assists, the highest total in the league. A record of six goals and two assists in nine Champions League games was particularly impressive for a playmaker who had only just turned 21 and would surely only get better with age and experience.

As Wenger himself said: 'So long as he does not suffer any major injuries, he could certainly be the best midfielder in the world.'

Next up for Fábregas was the Euro 2008 Championships

with Spain and a fight for a place in the starting 11, against stiff competition from former Barcelona team-mates Xavi and Iniesta, as well as Senna and Xabi Alonso. Before heading off for Austria and Switzerland, however, the Spaniard pledged his future to Arsenal, in the wake of growing interest from Inter Milan, Real Madrid and his former club Barcelona. Fábregas was confident about next season. He told the press: 'I think we will win something, of course.'

23

Narrow wins in warm-up matches against Peru and the USA did not mark Spain out as major threats in Euro 2008 but things were slowly coming together – and they did not want to reach their peak too early. Fábregas was extremely optimistic. He had learnt a lot from Spain's premature World Cup exit in Germany two years before and hoped to be given the chance to make amends. He badly wanted a place in the starting line-up.

However, Aragones seemed to prefer using Xavi and Senna in the centre of midfield with David Silva and Iniesta out wide. It meant that Spain were a little narrow at times but, with the rampaging runs of full-backs Sergio Ramos and Joan Capdevila, that was never a big concern.

Cesc watched from the touchline as his team-mates walked out to face Russia in their opening fixture in Group D. It promised to be a genuine test of Spain's credentials with some pundits tipping Russia to be the tournament's dark horses. But Guus Hiddink's side were simply swept aside by a Spanish performance full of flair, pace and movement. Villa was the star, finishing brilliantly to bag a hat-trick as his partnership with Torres continued to blossom. Fábregas entered the fray in the 54th minute for his European Championship debut. He instantly slotted into the team's patient passing style and helped leave the Russians floored. He capped a memorable afternoon by scoring his first international goal in the closing moments by heading home

Spain's fourth after Xavi's shot was parried. The game finished 4–1. Spain clearly meant business.

Cesc was given another second-half cameo in Spain's second group match against Sweden. Unsurprisingly, Aragones was reluctant to tinker with a winning formula but this was a sterner test. The Swedes fell behind to a Torres goal but did not wilt like the Russians had. Instead, they levelled through Ibrahimovic. Fábregas replaced Xavi with just over half an hour to go but found the Swedish rearguard tough to break down. It needed a last gasp Villa goal to snatch the points and leave Ibrahimovic and company stunned.

Six points out of six took the pressure off the final group game against Greece. With Aragones ringing the changes, Cesc was given his chance to show what he could do from the start of a match. Greece had nothing to play for but took the lead just before half-time. The Spanish second string had not clicked, yet a second-half fight back earned a 2–1 win, with Ruben De la Red and Daniel Guiza on target. Fábregas was not at his best but hoped that there would be more opportunities ahead.

The quarter-final against Italy surprisingly was a dire affair and Fábregas had to watch from the substitutes' bench. The Italians made little effort to craft chances, keeping men behind the ball. With Spain making limited impact, Cesc was thrown into the action just before the hour mark and he attempted to kick-start the team's passing style. The 90 minutes finished goalless, as did extra-time. And so two of the nations with the worst penalty-taking records headed into a shootout.

Spanish keeper Casillas pulled off saves from Daniele De Rossi and Antonio Di Natale, leaving Spain needing to score their final penalty to be sure of a place in the semi-finals. And that fifth taker was Fábregas. He marched up to the spot, probably the biggest moment of his career, kept his cool and fired the ball past Buffon. Spain were now just one match away from the final. Cesc later admitted to the media that he had not taken a penalty in a match since he was 15 and that he had changed his plan at the last minute.

The semi-finals produced a re-match with Russia. The rain poured down in Vienna and only one side came to the party. Fábregas started on the bench but entered the fray sooner than he could have possibly expected as Villa limped off. He played just behind Torres, looking for the killer pass.

The Russians, especially Andrei Arshavin, had dazzled Holland in the quarter final, but they surrendered limply in the second half against Fábregas and company. And it was Cesc who drove them to victory. He regularly found space to hurt the Russian back four and it was no surprise when Spain took a 50th-minute lead through Xavi.

Then Fábregas helped settle matters with a stunning pass for Guiza to double the lead. It was a pinpoint pass and summed up exactly what he brought to the team. And he was not finished yet. To rub salt into the Russians' wounds, he popped up with another fine assist as he laid on a third for Silva. Cesc had produced a play-making masterclass and the Spaniards were heading into the final.

There was just one hurdle left in their path. Germany had proved too strong for Turkey and it promised to be a very entertaining final. Villa's injury meant he was out but would Aragones select Cesc in his place? It seemed a no-brainer as the midfielder had stolen all the headlines with his display against Russia. And Aragones agreed; Fábregas would start in the Euro 2008 final.

The game began in a cagey fashion but Spain quickly appeared to have the measure of their opponents and their attacking pace was frightening the German defence. Fábregas found it hard to get into the match but joined in the celebrations in the 33rd minute as Torres' pace and endeavour gave Spain a vital lead. The striker shrugged off Philipp Lahm and dinked the ball over the advancing Lehmann.

Cesc dug in to help his team-mates protect the lead, without managing to find the type of passes that had cut Russia to shreds. He was replaced by Alonso just after the hour mark and, watched as Spain, who might have had Silva sent off, wasted several chances to extend the lead, but the Germans could not make them pay.

When the final whistle went, it was mayhem. Fábregas and his team-mates had won their first major title for 44 years and they celebrated in style. There had been some brilliant performances throughout the tournament. Senna had been phenomenal as a defensive midfield screen, Torres and Villa had been lethal up front and Casillas had been inspired at times. And of course Cesc had chipped in with some fine work of his own.

After the misery of walking past the Champions League trophy in 2006, Fábregas was ecstatic to be heading up for his winners medal and the chance to lift the big prize. He savoured the moment as Casillas raised the trophy and the celebrations carried on well into the night. The underachievers tag had been shed once and for all.

24

Back in England, a niggling hamstring injury kept Fábregas out of the vital pre-season training and he was still on the sidelines when they started their new campaign with a 1–0 win over West Brom. There was no doubt that his creative genius was missed in the centre of midfield and the Gunners had to manage without their talisman for a few more weeks as he struggled to shake off the injury. He didn't return to the starting line-up until late August against FC Twente when Arsenal won their Champions League qualifier and took their place in the group stage draw. The team were determined to make a good show in the competition and a 1–1 draw in Kiev was a decent start to the group stage. Drawn alongside Dynamo Kiev, Fenerbahce and Porto, the Gunners were hot favourites to top the group.

Their league form also looked good. They won five of their first six games with only two goals conceded but then they crashed to a shock 2–1 defeat against new boys Hull City. The team bounced back in midweek with a 4–0 win over Porto. Fábregas was still looking for his first goal of the season and he went close with a testing 20-yard strike. The goals would come but he was desperate to emulate his prolific start to last season. He finally got on target in dramatic fashion in the next game against Sunderland. The opposition took the lead with just four minutes to go. It looked like another defeat for the Gunners but in the last minute van Persie whipped in a corner and Fábregas rose to head the equaliser. The Gunners had barely deserved it but the Spaniard did not care as he celebrated jubilantly.

That triggered a run of good results, albeit with some unconvincing performances, with the Gunners beating Fenerbahce 5–2 in the Champions League and picking up 13 points from six league games. They included a 2–1 win over Manchester United and a thrilling 4–4 draw against Spurs. The only set back was a surprise 2–1 defeat at Stoke – Arsenal were definitely struggling to beat some of the lower clubs. But hoping to build on the momentum of the win over United, Arsenal now took on Aston Villa. They performed badly and Arsene Wenger was furious following the 2–0 defeat. 'It was a very bad afternoon because we were not sharp physically and beaten everywhere in the first half,' he complained.

Then came more controversy as Gallas decided to air some of his grievances publicly, complaining that teams were now being fearless when playing the Gunners and revealing tensions behind the scenes. He told the *Associated Press*: 'There was a problem at half-time of the 4–4 draw with Tottenham. The only thing I could say at half-time was, "guys, we resolve these problems after the match, not at half-time." When as captain some players come up to you and talk to you about a player... complaining about him... and then during the match you speak to this player and the player in question insults us, there comes a time where we can no longer comprehend how this can happen. I am trying to defend myself a bit without giving names. Otherwise I'm taking it all [the blame]. I'm 31, the player is six years younger than me.'

Cesc and his team-mates were stunned by the outburst and Wenger, who some felt ought to have been more decisive after some of Gallas' behaviour last season, was left with little choice but to take action. He dropped the French defender from the squad for the next match at Manchester City and stripped him of the captaincy.

Fábregas was frustrated to be suspended for the trip to City. He wanted to be there to help his team-mates at this worrying time. Almunia captained the side but it was another afternoon to forget, wrapping up a disastrous week for Arsenal. Robinho stole the show as City romped to a 3–0 victory.

It was a nightmare spell for everyone connected with the club but things picked up slightly for Cesc on the Monday when Wenger told reporters: 'Fábregas will be the captain permanently. I do not have to explain why. I believe the captain is the voice of the club towards the outside, and is one of the leaders of the team.'

A home fixture against Dynamo Kiev was just what Cesc and company needed. It appeared to be a relatively easy match but confidence was at such a low ebb that it was a major struggle. Fábregas led the way with a man of the match performance but Arsenal needed a goal in the 87th minute from Bendtner, who was picked out superbly by Cesc, to snatch the win.

Arsenal have never struggled to raise their game for the big matches and they once again proved this point with a gutsy performance against Chelsea, winning 2–1. However, a defeat to Porto in the Champions League consigned the Gunners to second place in the group and a potentially tougher second-round match. Then a trip to Middlesbrough reminded everyone that Fábregas and company still had plenty of improvements to make. Adebayor headed the side into the lead but Jeremie Aliadiere levelled and the Gunners dropped two more frustrating points.

However, Fábregas felt he was growing in confidence as captain and was looking ahead to the rest of the season when disaster struck. Arsenal clashed with Liverpool at the Emirates on 21 December and, just before half-time, Cesc and Alonso challenged for a loose ball in a tackle that left the Arsenal skipper writhing in agony. He was helped off the field at the break and would not return. The news was extremely bad: he would miss up to four months with ruptured knee ligaments. It left Fábregas and Arsenal shattered. The talisman was out of action and the new era, with the Spaniard running the show, was suddenly on hold. He told the press: 'It's the first serious injury that I've had in my career. Everyone gets injured and now it's my turn. My intention is to return as soon as possible to help my teammates and to do what I like most, to play football.'

It was 4 April before he returned. Arsenal were now in fourth place, 10 points behind the leaders Manchester United and six adrift of Liverpool and Chelsea. His comeback saw them beat Manchester City 2–0 and, even though their old habit of losing to lower clubs reared its head again with a 4–1 defeat at Wigan, there was still plenty to play for. A 4–1 aggregate win over Villreal put them into the semi-final of the Champions League, and their next match was an FA Cup semi-final against Chelsea.

The match was played at Wembley and the Gunners' hopes were raised when Theo Walcott fired them in front after just 18 minutes. Florent Malouda equalised after half an hour and the game was a tight stalemate with neither side able to create a clear-cut chance. But with four minutes to go Frank Lampard lobbed a ball forward and Didier Drogba raced on to it, rounded the keeper and tapped it home. Arsenal now only had one chance of silverware.

The first leg of the Champions League semi-final was at Old Trafford in front of more than 74,000 people. Manchester United were on top for long spells but they were restricted to a single goal, John O'Shea forcing home Michael Carrick's cross in the 17th minute. Fábregas kept driving his side forward at every opportunity and, in the dying minutes, he whipped in a dangerous free-kick but Nicklas Bendtner's header went over the bar.

Arsenal still fancied their chances when United came to the Emirates on 5 May. But the optimism only lasted 11 minutes, by which time the Gunners were 2–0 down. United stretched their lead in the second half and van Persie's late penalty, given when Darren Fletcher was harshly judged to have brought down Fábregas, was no consolation at all. Once more Arsenal had fallen short when in sight of a trophy.

The campaign finished with a 4–1 thrashing of Stoke but there was little to celebrate. Arsenal were again fourth, and this time 18 points behind Manchester United. Fábregas had been through a difficult season, marred by injury and with only three goals to his name. Once more he had nothing to show for his talent and while, as a fan, he celebrated Barcelona's Champions League triumph, he wouldn't have been human if he hadn't thought 'why wasn't I in that team?'

He returned to the Emirates for the start of the 2009-10 campaign which was to prove one of his most successful. With the extra responsibility of captaincy and a growing maturity, his talent was starting to flourish and he at last found the knack of scoring goals. He opened his account in a 4–0 win over Wigan and passed double figures at Christmas. With Andrei Arshavin wowing the Emirates fans, Fábregas no longer had the burden of being the wonderkid of the squad and it helped his game.

Arsenal continued to play some of the most attractive football in the Premiership, but they were still struggling to match the sides at the very top and were in danger of again failing to pick up any silverware. Inevitably rumours started to circulate that this would be Cesc's last season at the Emirates, even though it was reported that the Gunners were willing to make him the highest paid player in their history with a new deal worth £30 milllion.

Meanwhile, Fábregas aired his frustration when he told the *Daily Mail*: 'As a team we need to be stronger. We can't hide behind people saying we are too young or we have injuries. We just have to compete. People say you must learn from your mistakes, but you learn how to play football when you are 12. You don't learn these things when you are 25. The basics must be there. If you play for Arsenal, it is because you have to have these attributes. That is why I do not believe age is an excuse.'

And Arsenal fans wouldn't have been encouraged when they heard that their captain had told *Catalunya Radio*: 'Barcelona is the best city in the world to live in and the quality of life is great. I know it very well. I do not like the climate in London, but as a city it is spectacular. I have never hidden the fact that I want to return to Barcelona. Since I was nine months old, my grandfather would take me to the Barça stadium and all my life I have worn the Blaugrana colours. For one motive or another I had to go, but one never knows what can happen.'

It almost seems as though it is Fábregas's destiny to one day play for Barcelona at the Nou Camp. After all, he is one of Spain's most influential players as he showed when they impressively booked their place for the World Cup finals in South Africa.

25

Luis Argones had led Spain to their Euro 2008 triumph but now he was replaced by the former Real Madrid boss Vincente del Bosque. The new coach was charged with guiding his side to the World Cup finals in South Africa in the summer of 2010, and he had just a few weeks to prepare for the first qualifier at home to Bosnia-Herzegovina.

In 32 appearances, Cesc had played only five full games for his country and was hoping that a change of coach might mean a change of fortune, and it certainly seemed that way when he was named in the starting line up for the match in Murcia. David Villa had the Spanish fans anxiously chewing their nails when he missed a first-half penalty but he made amends early in the second half when he fired home Cesc's pinpoint pass. The night seemed to be going well for Fábregas but, after 65 minutes, he was substituted and clearly showed his frustration as he came off. Afterwards he was unrepentant saying, 'It's normal that you think like that when you've been taken off. The day they replace me and I'm not angry, I will leave football. It's not a lack of respect for anybody but wanting to be a better player every day.'

Del Bosque obviously didn't see it quite like that and dropped Fábregas to the bench for the next match, a comfortable 4–0 win over Armenia. The Arsenal midfielder finally came on in the 74th minute and provided the pass for Villa's second and Spain's third goal. That wasn't enough to get him back in the starting line-up for the next match and he only played a cameo role as Spain eased past Estonia 3–0.

It looked set to be another frustrating evening for the midfielder when he was on the bench for probably the hardest games so far, away to Belgium, but Fernando Torres was injured after 17 minutes and Fábregas took his place with Spain already trailing 1–0. Ten minutes before half time he provided the pass for Andres Iniesta to equalise and, two minutes from time, David Villa popped up with the winner. It had been an exhilarating but painful night for Fábregas who suffered a suspected broken nose but he was able to keep playing.

Spain were on a high and now Cesc and his team-mates got the feel of playing in South Africa in the Confederation Cup, winning their first four matches to give del Bosque 10 straight victories, the first international manager to achieve that from scratch. Victory over South Africa put them into the semi-final and gave them the world record of 15 consecutive wins and 35 matches unbeaten, but the run came to an unexpected halt when they went down 2–0 to the United States.

Injury kept Cesc out of the World Cup match against Turkey which saw Spain maintain their 100 per cent record in the qualifiers, but he was back on the bench in September 2009 when Spain thrashed Belgium 5–0. David Villa added two more to his tally – and missed another penalty – and the home side were already 3–0 when Cesc left the bench with 20 minutes to go. But he still made an impact, bringing a good diving save out of the Belgian keeper before setting up his country's final goal for Villa. Spain were six points clear with three matches to go. They had almost booked their ticket to South Africa.

They finished the job four days later, beating Estonia 3–0 while their only challengers, Bosnia-Herzegovina, drew with